200
SLOW COOKER
RECIPES

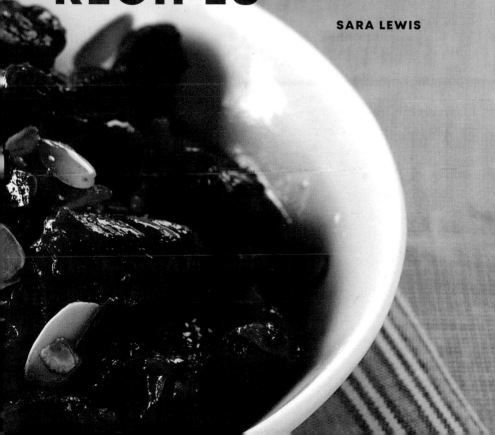

HAMLYN **ALL COLOR COOKBOOK**

200
SLOW COOKER
RECIPES

SARA LEWIS

An Hachette UK Company
www.hachette.co.uk

First published in Great Britain in 2009 by Hamlyn,
a division of Octopus Publishing Group Ltd,
Carmelite House, 50 Victoria Embankment,
London EC4Y 0DZ
www.octopusbooks.co.uk
www.octopusbooksusa.com

This edition published in 2019

Distributed in the US by Hachette Book Group,
1290 Avenue of the Americas, 4th and 5th Floors,
New York, NY 10104

Distributed in Canada by Canadian Manda Group,
664 Annette St., Toronto, Ontario, Canada M6S 2C8

ISBN 978-0-600-63621-2

Printed and bound in China

10 9 8 7 6 5 4 3 2 1

Standard level kitchen cup and spoon measurements are
used in all recipes.

Ovens should be preheated to the specific temperature; if
using a convection oven, follow manufacturer's instructions
for adjusting the time and the temperature.

Eggs should be large unless otherwise stated. The U.S.
Food and Drug Administration advises that eggs should
not be consumed raw. This book contains dishes made
with raw or lightly cooked eggs. Once prepared, these
dishes should be kept refrigerated and used promptly.

A few recipes contain nuts and nut derivatives.
Anyone with a known nut allergy must avoid these.

Read your slow cooker manual before you begin and
preheat the slow cooker if required according to the
manufacturer's instructions. Because slow cookers vary
slightly from manufacturer to manufacturer, check recipe
timings with the manufacturer's directions for a recipe
using the same ingredients.

All recipes for this book were tested in oval-shaped slow
cookers with a working capacity of 2.5 litres (4 pints)
and total capacity of 3.5 litres (6 pints) using metric
measurements. Where the slow cooker recipe is finished
off under the grill, hold the pot with teacloths to remove it
from the machine housing.

contents

introduction

introduction

If you want to prepare healthy, comforting meals but feel you just don't have time, then think again. As little as 15–20 minutes spent early in the day are all that are needed to prepare dinner for a slow cooker, leaving you free to get on with something else.

The slow cooker is ideal for anyone who has a young family because the dinner can be put on after the morning school run so that it is ready when you and the children are at your most tired at around 5.30 in the afternoon. If you work shifts or if you are a student with lectures during the day, you can put on a meal before you go out, so that dinner is waiting when you get back. If you are new to retirement, dinner can be left to cook while you enjoy a relaxing day at the golf course, or your slow cooker can leave you with the free time to tackle that home-repair project you've been putting off.

Because the food cooks so slowly, there is no need to worry about it boiling dry, spilling over, or burning on the bottom, and depending on the setting, it can be left for 8–10 hours. Food that has been slowly cooked has much more flavor than dishes prepared in other ways. When microwave ovens first came into use, they captured everyone's imagination as the answer to our busy working lives. And, yes, a microwave oven lets you cook food in minutes, but the reality is that the food is often tasteless and lacking in color. Frozen dinners are easy to prepare, but they, but they are somewhat lacking nutritionally and in flavor.

A slow cooker is environmentally friendly, too. There is no need to turn on the oven for just one dish when you can save fuel by using your slow cooker. It uses around the same amount of electricity as an electric light bulb, so they are cheap to run. In addition, the long, slow cooking transforms even the toughest and cheapest cuts of meat into dishes that melt in the mouth, and the meat will literally fall off the bone—try for example, Slow-Braised Pork with Ratatouille (pages 74–75) or Maple-Glazed Ribs (pages 90–91).

Slow cookers are perfect for steaming desserts, too. Because there is no evaporation you won't have to remember to fill up with water or return to find that the pot has boiled dry.

When water is added to the pot, it can also be used as a bain marie or water bath to cook baked custards, pâtés, or terrines. You can pour alcoholic or fruit juice mixtures into the pot and make warming hot party punches or hot toddies.

The slow cooker pot can also be used to make chocolate or cheese fondues, preserves (such as lemon curd or simple chutneys), and you can even boil bones or a chicken carcass to make into homemade stock.

size matters

Slow cookers are available in several sizes and are measured in capacity. The size usually printed on the packaging is the working capacity or the maximum space for food:

- For two people use a mini oval slow cooker with a maximum capacity of 1½ quarts and a working capacity of 1 quart.
- For four people choose a round or the more versatile oval cooker with a total capacity of 3½ quarts and a working capacity of 2½ quarts.
- For 6 people you will need a large oval slow cooker with a total capacity of 5 quarts and a working capacity of 4 quarts or the extra large round 6½ quarts with a working capacity of 4½ quarts.

Surprisingly, the very large slow cookers cost only a little more than the medium-size ones, and it is easy to be swept along thinking that they are a good buy. However, unless you have a large family or like to cook large quantities so that you have enough dinner for one meal with extra portions to freeze, you will probably find that they are too big for your everyday needs. Remember that you need to fill a slow cooker halfway when you are cooking meat, fish, or vegetable dishes.

The best and most versatile shape for a slow cooker is an oval, which is ideal for cooking a whole chicken and has ample room for an ovenproof dish or four individual custard cups and yet is capacious enough to make soup for six portions. Choose one with an indicator light so that you can see at a glance when the slow cooker is turned on.

9

before you start

It is important to read the manual before using your slow cooker. Some manufacturers recommend preheating the slow cooker on the high setting for a minimum of 20 minutes before food is added. Others recommend that it is heated only when filled with food.

how full should the pot be?

A slow cooker pot must be used only with the addition of liquid—ideally it should be no less than half full. Aim for the three-quarter full mark or, if you are making soups, make sure the liquid is no higher than 1 inch from the top.

Joints of meat should take up no more than two-thirds of the space. If you are using an ovenproof bowl, ensure there is ¾ inch space all the way around or ½ inch at the narrowest point if using an oval cooker.

heat settings

All slow cookers have a "high", "low" and "off" setting, and some also have either "medium", "warm" or "auto" settings. In general, the "high" setting will take only half the time of the "low" setting when you are cooking a diced meat or vegetable casserole. This can be useful if you plan to eat at lunchtime or are delayed in starting the casserole. Both settings will reach just below 212°F, boiling point, during cooking, but when it is set to "high" the temperature is reached more quickly.

A combination of settings can be useful and is recommended by some manufacturers at the beginning of cooking. See your manufacturer's manual for more details.

what is best at what setting?

Following is a general guide to what you should cook at which temperature.

low

- Diced meat or vegetable casseroles
- Chops or chicken joints
- Soups
- Egg custard desserts
- Rice dishes
- Fish dishes

high

- Sweet or savory steamed puddings or sweet dishes that include a raising agent (either self-rising flour or baking powder).
- Pâtés or terrines.
- Whole chicken, guinea fowl, or pheasant, ham steak or half a shoulder of lamb.

timings

All the recipes in the book have variable timings, which means that they will be tender and ready to eat at the lower time but can be left without spoiling for an extra hour or two, which is perfect if you are delayed at work or stuck in traffic.

If you want to speed up or slow down casseroles based on diced meat or vegetables so that the cooking fits around your plans better, adjust the heat settings and timings as suggested below:

Low	Medium	High
6–8 hours	4–6 hours	3–4 hours
8–10 hours	6–8 hours	5–6 hours
10–12 hours	8–10 hours	7–8 hours

(The above timings were taken from the Morphy Richards slow cooker instruction manual. Note: Do not change timings or settings for fish, whole joints, or dairy dishes.)

using your slow cooker for the first time

Before you start to use the slow cooker, put it on the countertop, somewhere out of the way, and make sure that the cord is tucked around the back of the machine and not trailing over the front of the counter.

The outside of the slow cooker does get hot, so warn young members of the family

and don't forget to wear oven mitts or use dish towels when you are lifting the pot out of the housing. Set it onto a heatproof mat on the table or countertop to serve the food.

If your slow cooker lid has a vent in the top, make sure that the slow cooker is not put under an eye-level cabinet or the steam may catch someone's arm as they reach into the cabinet.

Always check that the joint, ovenproof dish, soufflé dish, or individual ramekins will fit into your slow cooker pot before you begin work on a recipe to avoid frustration when you get to a critical point.

preparing food for the slow cooker

meat

Cut meat into pieces that are the same size so that cooking is even, and fry meat before adding to the slow cooker.

A whole guinea fowl or pheasant, a small ham steak, or half a shoulder of lamb can be cooked in an oval slow cooker pot, but make sure that it does not fill more than the lower

tip
As the slow cooker heats up, it forms a water seal just under the lid, but whenever you lift the lid you break the seal. For each time you lift the lid, add 20 minutes to the cooking time.

two-thirds of the pot. Cover it with boiling liquid and cook on high. Check it is cooked either by using a meat thermometer or by inserting a skewer through the thickest part and checking that the juices run clear.

Add boiling stock or sauce to the slow cooker pot and press the meat beneath the surface before cooking begins.

vegetables

Root vegetables can (surprisingly) take longer to cook than meat. If you are adding vegetables to a meat casserole, make sure you cut them into pieces that are a little smaller than the meat and try to keep all the vegetable chunks the same size so that they cook evenly. Press the vegetables and the meat below the surface of the liquid before cooking begins.

When you are making soup, puree it while it is still in the slow cooker pot by using an immersion hand blender if you have one.

fish

Whether you cut the fish into pieces or cook it in a larger piece of about 1 lb, the slow, gentle cooking will not cause the fish to break up or overcook. Make sure that the fish is covered by the hot liquid so that it cooks evenly right through to the center.

Do not add shellfish to the pot until the last 15 minutes of cooking, and make sure that the slow cooker is set to high. If the fish was frozen, it must be thoroughly thawed, rinsed with cold water, and drained before use.

---

tip
You can make so much more than just a casserole in the slow cooker. Try soups, steamed puddings, baked custards, hot toddies, and even cakes, chutneys, and preserves.

---

pasta

For best results, cook the pasta separately in a saucepan of boiling water and then mix with the casserole just before serving. Small pasta shapes, such as macaroni or shells, can be added to soups 30–45 minutes before the end of cooking.

Pasta can be soaked in boiling water for short-cook recipes, such as Macaroni with Smoked Haddock (see pages 132–33).

rice

Instant rice is preferable for slow cookers because it has been partially cooked during manufacture and some of the starch has been washed off, making it less sticky.

When you are cooking rice, allow a minimum of 1 cup water for each 1 cup of instant rice or up to 2 cups for risotto rice.

dried beans and lentils

Make sure that you soak dried beans in plenty of cold water overnight. Drain them, then put them into a saucepan with fresh water and bring to a boil. Boil rapidly for 10 minutes, then drain or add with the cooking liquid to the slow cooker. See the recipes for details.

Pearl barley, lentils—red or green—do not need soaking overnight. If you are unsure, check the instructions on the package.

cream and milk

Both cream and milk are generally added at the beginning of cooking only when you are making rice pudding or baked egg custard-style dishes. Use whole milk where milk is cooked directly in the cooker pot rather than ramekins because it is less likely to separate.

If you are making soup, add the milk at the very end, after the soup has been pureed. Stir cream into soups just 15 minutes before the end of cooking.

thickening stews and casseroles

Casseroles can be thickened in just the same way as if you were cooking conventionally. You can do it either before slow cooking, by adding the flour after searing meat or frying onions, or you can thicken the casserole with cornstarch mixed with a little water 30–60 minutes before the end of cooking.

adapting your own recipes

If you have a favorite recipe that you would like to make in your slow cooker, look at a similar recipe in this book to give you an idea of the quantity that will fit into the slow cooker pot and the appropriate timing for the main ingredient. Because a slow cooker cooks food so gently and evenly, you will find that you need to reduce the amount of liquid. Begin by using just half the amount of hot liquid, and then add to it as needed, pressing foods beneath the surface of the liquid and increasing the amount until just covered. Recipes that contain fresh tomatoes will turn to pulp during cooking, so you will not need quite so much liquid.

In the slow cooker, the steam condenses on the lid and returns to the pot, so there is no danger of recipes boiling dry. If you find

you have reduced the amount of liquid too much, add a little more boiling stock or water at the end of cooking to compensate.

It is usually best to add milk or cream at the end of the recipe unless the recipe uses the slow cooker pot as a bain marie or water bath, when hot water is poured around a cooking dish. Rice pudding and porridge is the exception to this, and you should use long-life, UHT or whole milk and not low-fat or skim milk for these. Refer to individual recipes in the book for guidance.

When you are adapting a recipe remember:
- Foods cooked in a slow cooker must contain some liquid.
- Foods will not brown during cooking, so fry foods before they go in or brown the top by transferring the slow cooker pot from its housing to the broiler just before serving or by using a cook's blowtorch.

changing recipes to suit a different model

All the recipes in this book have been tested in a standard-size slow cooker with a total capacity of 3½ quarts. You might have a larger 5 quart six-portion-size cooker or a tiny

1½ quart two-portion cooker, and to adapt the recipes in this book you can simply halve for two portions or add half as much again to the recipe for more portions, keeping the timings the same. All those recipes made in an ovenproof dish, soufflé dish, or individual molds or cups, may also be cooked in a larger slow cooker for the same amount of time.

for the freezer

The majority of soups and stews in this book can be frozen successfully, and if you do not have a large family or if you live on your own, freezing individual portions for another meal can be a great time saver. After all, it requires only a little extra effort to make a casserole for four than it does to make one for two. Defrost portions in the refrigerator overnight or at room temperature for 4 hours, then reheat

thoroughly in a saucepan on the stove top or in the microwave on full power.

If you are using raw frozen foods, make sure that they are thoroughly thawed before you add them to the slow cooker. Exceptions to this rule are frozen peas and corn. Raw food that was frozen and is then thawed and cooked in the slow cooker can be refrozen in its cooked and cooled state.

caring for your slow cooker

If you look after it carefully, you may find that your machine lasts for 20 years or more.

Because the heat of a slow cooker is so controllable it is not like a saucepan with burned-on grime to contend with. Simply lift the slow cooker pot out of the housing, fill it with hot soapy water, and let it soak for a while. Although it is tempting to put the slow cooker pot and lid into the dishwasher, they do take up a lot of space, and check with your manual first, because not all are dishwasher proof.

Let the machine itself cool down before cleaning. Turn it off at the controls and pull out the plug. Wipe the inside with a damp dish cloth, removing any stubborn marks with a little cream cleaner. The outside of the machine and the controls can be wiped with a dish cloth, then buffed up with a duster or, if it has a chrome-effect finish, sprayed with a little multisurface cleaner and polished with a duster. **Never immerse the machine in water to clean it.** If you are storing the slow cooker in a cabinet, make sure it is completely cold before you put it away.

> **tip**
> So that you can easily lift a hot bowl out of the slow cooker, tear off two long pieces of foil. Fold each into thirds to make a long, thin strap. Put one on top of the other to make a cross, then sit the ovenproof bowl in the center. Lift up the straps, then lower the bowl into the slow cooker pot carefully. Alternatively, you can buy slow cooker liner bags, but do make sure that they will comfortably hold a 1¼ quart bowl before you buy one.

breakfasts
& light bites

banana & cinnamon porridge

Preparation time **5 minutes**
Cooking temperature **low**
Cooking time **1–2 hours**
Serves **4**

2½ cups boiling **water**
1¼ cups **long life (UHT) milk**
1¾ cups **rolled oats**
2 **bananas**
¼ cup **light** or **dark brown
sugar**
¼ teaspoon **ground cinnamon**

Preheat the slow cooker, if necessary; see the manufacturer's instructions. Pour the boiling water and milk into the slow cooker pot, then stir in the oats.

Cover with the lid and cook on low for 1 hour for thin porridge or 2 hours for thick porridge.

Spoon into bowls, slice the bananas, and divide among the bowls. Mix together the sugar and cinnamon and sprinkle over the top.

For hot spiced muesli, follow the recipe as above, adding 2 cups Swiss-style muesli. When cooked, stir in ¼ teaspoon ground cinnamon and top with ½ cup diced, dried apricots. Drizzle over 2 tablespoons honey before serving.

eggs en cocotte with salmon

Preparation time **10 minutes**
Cooking temperature **high**
Cooking time **40–45 minutes**
Serves **4**

2 tablespoons **butter**
4 **eggs**
¼ cup **heavy cream**
2 teaspoons chopped **chives**
1 teaspoon chopped **tarragon**
7 oz **smoked salmon**, sliced
salt and **black pepper**
4 **lemon wedges**, to garnish
4 slices **toast**, to serve

Preheat the slow cooker, if necessary; see the manufacturer's instructions. Liberally butter the inside of 4 heatproof porcelain ramekin dishes, each ⅔ cup and break an egg into each ramekin.

Drizzle the cream over the eggs and sprinkle over the herbs and a little salt and black pepper. Transfer the ramekins to the slow cooker pot and pour boiling water into the pot to come halfway up the sides of the ramekins.

Cover with the lid (there is no need to cover the dishes with foil) and cook on high for 40–45 minutes or until the egg whites are set and the yolks still slightly soft.

Lift the dishes carefully out of the slow cooker pot with a dish towel, transfer to plates, and serve with smoked salmon, lemon wedges, and triangles of toast.

For spiced eggs en cocotte, break the eggs into buttered dishes and drizzle over each 1 tablespoon heavy cream, a few drops of Tabasco sauce, and a little salt and black pepper. Sprinkle 3 teaspoons finely chopped cilantro over the dishes and bake as above. Serve with toast and thin slices of pastrami.

easy sausage & beans

Preparation time **15 minutes**
Cooking temperature **low**
Cooking time **9–10 hours** or
 overnight
Serves **4**

1 tablespoon **sunflower oil**
1 **onion**, chopped
½ teaspoon **smoked paprika**
 (pimenton)
3¼ cups (28 oz can)
 baked beans
2 teaspoons **whole-grain
 mustard**
2 tablespoons **Worcestershire
 sauce**
6 tablespoons **vegetable
 stock**
2 **tomatoes**, roughly chopped
½ **red bell pepper**, cored,
 seeded, and diced
11½ oz chilled **frankfurters**,
 thickly sliced
salt and **black pepper**
buttered **toast**, to serve

Preheat the slow cooker, if necessary; see the manufacturer's instructions. Heat the oil in a skillet, add the onion, and fry, stirring, for 5 minutes or until softened and just beginning to turn golden.

Stir in the paprika and cook for 1 minute, then mix in the beans, mustard, Worcestershire sauces, and stock. Bring to the boil, then stir in the tomatoes, red bell pepper and a little salt and black pepper.

Add the frankfurters to the slow cooker pot and tip the baked bean mixture over the top. Cover with the lid and cook on low for 9–10 hours or overnight.

Stir well, then spoon into shallow bowls and serve with buttered toast fingers.

For chilied sausage & beans, add ½ teaspoon crushed dried red chilies, ¼ teaspoon cumin seeds, roughly crushed in a mortar and pestle, and a pinch of ground cinnamon to the smoked paprika and fried onion. Omit the mustard and Worcestershire sauce, then continue as above, adding the beans, stock, tomatoes, red bell pepper and frankfurters. Cook on low for 9–10 hours.

vanilla breakfast dried plums & figs

Preparation time **5 minutes**
Cooking temperature **low**
Cooking time **8–10 hours** or
   overnight
Serves **4**

1 **breakfast tea** teabag
2½ cups boiling **water**
⅔ cup pitted **dried plums**
   (prunes)
¾ cup dried **figs**
⅛ cup **superfine sugar**
1 teaspoon **vanilla extract**
pared rind of ½ **orange**

To serve
plain **yogurt**
muesli

Preheat the slow cooker if necessary; see the manufacturer's instructions. Put the teabag into a pitcher or teapot, add the boiling water, and let to soak for 2–3 minutes. Remove the teabag and pour the tea into the slow cooker pot.

Add the whole dried plums (prunes) and figs, the sugar, and vanilla extract to the hot tea, sprinkle with the orange rind, and mix together. Cover with the lid and cook on low for 8–10 hours or overnight.

Serve hot with spoonfuls of plain yogurt and a sprinkling of muesli.

For breakfast apricots in orange, put 1¾ cups dried apricots, ¼ cup superfine sugar, 1¼ cups boiling water, and ⅔ cup orange juice in the slow cooker pot. Cover and cook as above.

big breakfast bonanza

Preparation time **20 minutes**
Cooking temperature **low**
Cooking time **9–10 hours** or
  overnight
Serves **4**

1 tablespoon **sunflower oil**
12 **herby cocktail sausages**,
  about 13 oz in total
1 **onion**, thinly sliced
4 medium (1 lb) **potatoes**,
  peeled and cut into 1 inch
  chunks
2 cups roughly chopped
  tomatoes
4 oz **blood sausage**, peeled
  and cut into chunks
1 cup **vegetable stock**
2 tablespoons **Worcestershire
  sauce**
1 teaspoon **English mustard**
2–3 stems of **thyme**, plus
  extra to garnish
salt and **black pepper**

To serve
slices of **white bread**
  (optional)
4 poached **eggs** (optional)

Preheat the slow cooker, if necessary; see the manufacturer's instructions. Heat the oil in a skillet, add the cocktail sausages, and brown on one side, turn, and add the onion. Fry, turning the sausages and stirring the onions until the sausages are browned but not cooked.

Add the potatoes, tomatoes, and blood sausage to the slow cooker pot. Lift the cocktail sausages and onion from the skillet with a slotted spoon and transfer to the slow cooker pot. Pour off the excess fat, then add the stock, Worcestershire sauce, and mustard. Tear the leaves from the thyme stems and add to the skillet with some salt and black pepper.

Bring to a boil and pour over the sausages in the pot. Press the potatoes down so that the liquid covers them. Cover with the lid and cook on low for 9–10 hours or overnight. Stir before serving and garnish with extra thyme leaves. Serve with slices of white bread or a poached egg.

For a vegetarian big breakfast, fry 13 oz meat-free sausages in the oil with the onion as above. Add the potatoes and tomatoes to the slow cooker pot with 1¾ cups halved white mushrooms instead of the blood sausage. Heat the stock with the mustard and thyme and add 1 tablespoon tomato paste instead of the Worcestershire sauce. Season with salt and black pepper, then pour the mixture over the sausages in the slow cooker. Cover and cook as above.

cajun red bean soup

Preparation time **25 minutes**,
  plus overnight soaking
Cooking temperature **low**
Cooking time **8½–10½ hours**
Serves **6**

⅔ cup **dried red kidney
  beans**, soaked overnight in
  cold water
2 tablespoons **sunflower oil**
1 large **onion**, chopped
1 **red bell pepper**, cored,
  seeded, and diced
1 **carrot**, diced
1 **baking potato**, diced
2–3 **garlic cloves**, chopped
  (optional)
2 teaspoons mixed **Cajun
  spice** or ½–1 teaspoon
  chili powder
13 oz canned **chopped
  tomatoes**
1 tablespoon **brown sugar**
4¼ cups hot **vegetable stock**
4 **okra**, sliced
½ cup **green beans**, cut into
  short lengths
salt and **black pepper**

Preheat the slow cooker, if necessary; see the manufacturer's instructions. Drain and rinse the soaked beans, add to a saucepan, cover with fresh water, and bring to a boil. Boil vigorously for 10 minutes, then drain into a strainer.

Meanwhile, heat the oil in a large skillet. Add the onion and fry, stirring, for 5 minutes or until softened. Add the red bell pepper, carrot, potato, and garlic (if used) and fry for 2–3 minutes. Stir in the Cajun spice, tomatoes, sugar, and plenty of salt and black pepper and bring to the boil.

Transfer the mixture to the slow cooker pot, add the drained beans and hot stock, and mix together. Cover with the lid and cook on low for 8–10 hours.

Add the green vegetables, replace the lid, and cook for 30 minutes. Ladle the soup into bowls and serve with crusty bread, if liked.

For Hungarian paprika & red bean soup, make up the soup as above but add 1 teaspoon smoked paprika instead of the Cajun spice. Cook as above, omitting the green vegetables. Puree, return to the slow cooker and top up with a little boiling water if needed. Ladle into soup bowls, top each with 2 tablespoons sour cream and a few caraway seeds, and serve.

chili black bean stew

Preparation time **30 minutes**,
  plus overnight soaking
Cooking temperature **low**
Cooking time **8–10 hours**
Serves **4–6**

1⅓ cups **dried black beans**,
  soaked overnight in cold
  water
2 tablespoons **olive oil**
1 large **onion**, chopped
2 **carrots**, diced
2 **celery ribs**, sliced
2–3 **garlic cloves**, chopped
1 teaspoon **fennel seeds**,
  crushed
1 teaspoon **cumin seeds**,
  crushed
2 teaspoons **coriander seeds**,
  crushed
1 teaspoon **chili powder** or
  smoked paprika (pimenton)
13 oz canned **chopped
  tomatoes**
1¼ cups **vegetable stock**
1 tablespoon **brown sugar**
⅔ cup **sour cream** or **plain
  yogurt** (optional)
salt and **black pepper**
boiled **rice** or crusty **bread**,
  to serve

Preheat the slow cooker, if necessary; see the manufacturer's instructions. Drain and rinse the soaked beans. Place them in a saucepan, add fresh water to cover, and bring to the boil. Boil vigorously for 10 minutes, then drain into a strainer.

Meanwhile, heat the oil in a saucepan, add the onion, and fry, stirring, for 5 minutes or until softened. Add the carrots, celery, and garlic and fry for 2–3 minutes. Stir the crushed fennel, cumin, and coriander seeds into the vegetables with the chili powder and cook for 1 minute.

Add the tomatoes, stock, sugar, and a little black pepper. Bring to a boil, then pour into the slow cooker pot. Mix in the beans, pressing them under the liquid, then cover with the lid and cook on low for 8–10 hours.

Season the cooked beans to taste with salt. Top with spoonfuls of sour cream or yogurt and avocado salsa (see below) and serve accompanied by boiled rice or crusty bread.

For avocado salsa to accompany the stew halve an avocado and remove the pit and skin. Dice the flesh, and toss with the grated rind and juice of 1 lime. Mix with ½ finely chopped red onion, 2 diced tomatoes, and 2 tablespoons chopped cilantro leaves. Make the salsa about 10 minutes before serving the stew.

chicken & noodle broth

Preparation time **10 minutes**
Cooking temperature **high**
Cooking time **5 hours**
  20 minutes–7½ hours
Serves **4**

1 **chicken** carcass
1 **onion**, cut into wedges
2 **carrots**, sliced
2 **celery ribs**, sliced
1 **bouquet garni**
5 cups boiling **water**
3 oz **vermicelli pasta**
¼ cup chopped **parsley**
salt and **black pepper**

Preheat the slow cooker, if necessary; see the manufacturer's instructions. Put the chicken carcass into the slow cooker pot, breaking it into 2 pieces if necessary to make it fit. Add the onion, carrots, celery, and bouquet garni.

Pour over the boiling water and add a little salt and black pepper. Cover with the lid and cook on high for 5–7 hours.

Strain the soup into a large strainer, then quickly pour the hot soup back into the slow cooker pot. Take any meat off the carcass and add to the pot. Taste and adjust the seasoning, if needed. Add the pasta and cook on high for 20–30 minutes or until the pasta is just cooked. Sprinkle with parsley and ladle into deep bowls. Serve with warm bread, if liked.

For chicken & minted pea soup, make up the soup base as above, then strain and pour it back into the slow cooker. Add 2¼ cups finely sliced leeks, 2½ cups frozen peas, and a small bunch of mint, cover, and cook on high for 30 minutes. Mash or puree with an immersion hand blender, then stir in 5 oz mascarpone cheese until melted. Ladle into bowls and sprinkle with extra mint leaves, if liked.

smoked salmon timbales

Preparation time **30 minutes**,
   plus chilling
Cooking temperature **low**
Cooking time **3–3½ hours**
Serves **4**

butter for greasing
1 cup **crème fraîche** (or ½ cup
   sour cream mixed with ½ cup
   whipping cream)
4 egg yolks
grated rind and juice of
   ½ **lemon**
1 small bunch of **basil**
3½ oz sliced **smoked salmon**
salt and **black pepper**
lemon wedges, to garnish

Preheat the slow cooker, if necessary; see the manufacturer's instructions. Lightly butter 4 individual metal molds, each ⅔ cup, and line the bottoms with circles of nonstick parchment or wax paper.

Put the crème fraîche in a bowl and gradually beat in the egg yolks. Add the lemon rind and juice and season with salt and black pepper. Chop half of the basil and 3 oz of the smoked salmon, then stir both into the crème fraîche mixture.

Pour the mixture into the prepared molds. Stand the molds in the slow cooker pot (there is no need to cover them with foil). Pour hot water around the molds to come halfway up the sides, cover with the lid, and cook on low for 3–3½ hours or until the molds are set.

Remove the molds carefully from the slow cooker using a dish towel and let cool at room temperature. Transfer to the refrigerator and chill for at least 4 hours or overnight.

Loosen the edges of the timbales with a knife dipped in hot water, then invert onto serving plates and remove the molds. Smooth any rough areas with the side of the knife and remove the lining paper. Top with the remaining smoked salmon and basil leaves and garnish with lemon wedges.

For smoked mackerel timbales, omit the basil and smoked salmon and stir in 3 tablespoons freshly chopped chives, ½ teaspoon hot horseradish, and 3 oz skinned, flaked smoked mackerel fillets. Continue as above. Serve with salad.

gingered sweet potato soup

Preparation time **30 minutes**
Cooking temperature **low** and **high**
Cooking time **6¼–8¼ hours**
Serves **6**

1 tablespoon **olive oil**
1 **onion**, chopped
2 **garlic cloves**, finely chopped
1 teaspoon **fennel seeds**, crushed
1½ inch **fresh ginger**, peeled and finely chopped
3¾ cups **vegetable stock**
2 large (1 lb) **sweet potatoes**, diced
¾ cup **red lentils**
1¼ cups **whole milk**
salt and **black pepper**
warm **naan**, to serve

To garnish
2 tablespoons **olive oil**
1 **onion**, thinly sliced
1 teaspoon **fennel seeds**, crushed
½ teaspoon **ground cumin**
¼ teaspoon **ground turmeric**
1 teaspoon **superfine sugar**

Preheat the slow cooker, if necessary; see the manufacturer's instructions. Heat the oil in a large skillet, add the onion, and fry, stirring, for 5 minutes or until lightly browned. Add the garlic, fennel seeds, and ginger and cook for 2 minutes. Add the stock and salt and black pepper and bring to a boil.

Put the sweet potatoes and lentils in the slow cooker pot, pour over the hot stock mixture, cover with the lid, and cook on low for 6–8 hours or until the potatoes and lentils are soft.

Puree the soup, in batches if necessary, and return it to the slow cooker. Stir in the milk and cook on high for 15 minutes.

Meanwhile, make the garnish. Heat the oil in a clean skillet, add the onion, and fry over a low heat, stirring occasionally, for 10 minutes or until softened. Stir in the spices and sugar, increase the heat slightly, and fry for 5 more minutes or until golden brown.

Ladle the soup into bowls and sprinkle the spicy onions over the top. Serve with warm naan.

For curried red lentil & carrot soup, fry the onion and garlic in oil as above. Omit the seeds and ginger and instead add 4 teaspoons balti curry paste (or a curry paste of your choice). Cook for 2 minutes, then mix in vegetable stock and lentils, adding 8 medium diced carrots instead of the sweet potatoes. Continue as above, serving with a swirl of yogurt instead of the fried onion mix.

potato, apple & bacon hotchpotch

Preparation time **20 minutes**
Cooking temperature **low**
Cooking time **9–10 hours** or
   overnight
Serves **4**

6 medium (1½ lb) **potatoes**,
   thinly sliced
2 tablespoons **butter**
1 tablespoon **sunflower oil**
2 **onions**, roughly chopped
8 oz **smoked lean bacon**,
   diced
1 **apple**, cored and sliced
2 tablespoons **all-purpose
   flour**
2 cups **chicken stock**
2 teaspoons **English mustard**
2 **bay leaves**
½ cup shredded **cheddar
   cheese**
salt and **black pepper**

Preheat the slow cooker, if necessary; see the
manufacturer's instructions. Bring a large saucepan
of water to a boil, add the potatoes, and cook for
3 minutes, then drain.

Heat the butter and oil in a skillet, add the onions
and bacon, and fry, stirring, for 5 minutes or until just
beginning to turn golden. Stir in the apple and flour and
season the mixture well.

Layer the potatoes and the onion mixture alternately
in the slow cooker pot, ending with a layer of potatoes.
Bring the stock and mustard to a boil in the skillet, then
pour into the slow cooker pot and add the bay leaves.
Cover with the lid and cook on low for 9–10 hours.

Sprinkle the top of the potatoes with the cheese, lift
the pot out of the housing using oven mitts and brown
under the broiler, if liked, then spoon into shallow bowls.
Serve with broiler tomato halves sprinkled with chopped
chives, if liked.

For cidered chicken & bacon hotchpotch, blanch the
potatoes as above, then fry the onions with 4 oz diced
smoked lean bacon and 4 diced, boneless and skinless
chicken thighs. Stir in the apple, flour, and seasoning,
then layer in the slow cooker pot with the potatoes. Heat
1¼ cups chicken stock, ⅔ cup dry hard cider, and the
mustard and continue as above. Serve as a supper dish.

caldo verde

Preparation time **20 minutes**

Cooking temperature **low and high**

Cooking time **6¼ hours– 8 hours 20 minutes**

Serves **6**

2 tablespoons **olive oil**

2 **onions**, chopped

2 **garlic cloves**, finely chopped

5 oz **chorizo** in one piece, skinned and diced

3 small (1¼ lb) **baking potatoes**, cut into ½ inch dice

1 teaspoon **smoked paprika** (pimenton)

5 cups hot **chicken stock**

1⅓ cups finely shredded **green cabbage**

salt and **black pepper**

Preheat the slow cooker, if necessary; see the manufacturer's instructions. Heat the oil in a large skillet, add the onions, and fry, stirring, for 5 minutes or until lightly browned. Add the garlic, chorizo, potatoes, and paprika and cook for 2 minutes.

Transfer the mixture to the slow cooker pot, add the hot stock, and season to taste with salt and black pepper. Cover with the lid and cook on low for 6–8 hours.

Add the cabbage, replace the lid, and cook on high for 15–20 minutes or until the cabbage is tender. Ladle the soup into bowls and serve with warm, crusty bread, if liked.

For caldo verde with pumpkin, prepare the soup as above, reducing the baking potatoes to 2 small (12 oz) and adding 2 cups peeled, seeded, and diced pumpkin. Reduce the chicken stock to 3¾ cups and add a 13 oz can chopped tomatoes.

beery cheese fondue

Preparation time **15 minutes**
Cooking temperature **high**
Cooking time **40–60 minutes**
Serves **4**

1 tablespoon **butter**
2 **shallots** or ½ small **onion**,
  finely chopped
1 **garlic clove**, finely chopped
3 teaspoons **cornstarch**
1 can **blonde beer** or **lager**
1¾ cups shredded **Gruyère
  cheese**
1½ cups shredded **Swiss
  cheese**
grated **nutmeg**
salt and **black pepper**

To serve
½ whole-wheat **French bread**,
  cubed
2 **celery ribs**, cut into short
  lengths
8 small **pickled onions**,
  drained and halved
1 bunch of **radishes**, tops
  trimmed
1 **red bell pepper**, cored,
  seeded, and cubed
2 **heads chicory**, leaves
  separated

Preheat the slow cooker, if necessary; see the manufacturer's instructions. Butter the inside of the slow cooker pot, then add the shallots or onion and garlic.

Put the cornstarch in a small bowl and mix with a little of the beer to make a smooth paste, then blend with the remaining beer. Add to the slow cooker with both cheeses, a little nutmeg, and some salt and black pepper.

Stir together, then cover with the lid and cook on high for 40–60 minutes, whisking once during cooking. Whisk again and serve with the dippers arranged on a serving plate, with long fondue or ordinary forks for dunking the dippers into the fondue.

For classic cheese fondue, omit the beer from the above ingredients and add ¾ cup dry white wine and 1 tablespoon Kirsch. Cook as above and serve with bread to dip.

chunky chickpea & chorizo soup

Preparation time **20 minutes**
Cooking temperature **low**
Cooking time **6–8 hours**
Serves **4**

2 tablespoons **olive oil**
1 **onion**, chopped
2 **garlic cloves**, finely
    chopped
5 oz **chorizo**, skinned and
    diced
¾ teaspoon **smoked paprika**
    (pimenton)
2–3 stems **thyme**
4¼ cups **chicken stock**
1 tablespoon **tomato paste**
2¾ cups diced **sweet**
    potatoes
13½ oz canned **chickpeas**
    (garbanzo beans), drained
salt and **black pepper**
chopped **parsley** or extra
    thyme leaves, to garnish

Preheat the slow cooker, if necessary; see the
manufacturer's instructions. Heat the oil in a skillet,
add the onion, and fry, stirring, for 5 minutes or until
just beginning to turn golden.

Stir in the garlic and chorizo and cook for 2 minutes.
Mix in the paprika, add the thyme, stock, and tomato
paste, and bring to a boil, stirring, then add a little salt
and black pepper.

Add the sweet potatoes and chickpeas to the slow
cooker pot and pour over the hot stock mixture. Cover
with the lid and cook on low for 6–8 hours, until the
sweet potatoes are tender.

Ladle into bowls, sprinkle with a little chopped parsley
or extra thyme, and serve with warm pita breads,
if liked.

For tomato, chickpea & chorizo soup, make the
soup as above up to the point where the paprika
and thyme have been added. Reduce the stock to
3 cups and add to the skillet with the tomato paste
and 2 teaspoons brown sugar. Bring to a boil. Omit
the sweet potatoes but add 3 medium (1 lb) skinned
and diced tomatoes to the slow cooker pot along
with the chickpeas. Pour over the stock mixture and
continue as above.

brandied duck & walnut terrine

Preparation time **45 minutes**,
plus overnight chilling
Cooking temperature **high**
Cooking time **5–6 hours**
Serves **6**

6 oz rindless **smoked fatty
    bacon** slices
1 tablespoon **olive oil**
1 **onion**, chopped
2 boneless **sparerib pork
    chops**, about 9 oz
    in total
2 boneless **duck breasts**,
    about 12 oz in total, fat
    removed
2 **garlic cloves**, chopped
3 tablespoons **brandy**
1⅔ cups **fresh bread crumbs**
⅓ cup drained **sun-dried
    tomatoes** in oil, chopped
3 **pickled walnuts**, drained
    and roughly chopped
1 **egg**, beaten
1 tablespoon **green black
    peppercorns**, roughly
    crushed
salt

Preheat the slow cooker, if necessary; see the manufacturer's instructions. Lay the bacon slices on a cutting board and stretch each one, using the flat of a large cook's knife, until half as long again. Line the bottom and sides of a 6 inch diameter, deep, heatproof soufflé dish with bacon.

Heat the oil in a skillet, add the onion and fry, stirring, for 5 minutes. Finely chop or grind the pork and 1 of the duck breasts. Cut the second duck breast into long, thin slices and set aside. Stir the garlic and ground or chopped meat into the pan and cook for 3 minutes. Add the brandy, flame with a match, and stand well back until the flames subside.

Stir in the remaining ingredients. Mix well, then press half the mixture into the bacon-lined dish. Top with the sliced duck, then add the remaining mixture. Fold the bacon ends over the top, adding any leftover slices to cover the gaps. Cover with foil.

Place the dish on an upturned saucer in the bottom of the slow cooker pot. Pour boiling water around the dish to come halfway up the sides. Cover with the lid and cook on high for 5–6 hours or until the meat juices run clear when the center of the terrine is pierced with a knife.

Lift the dish carefully out of the pot using a dish towel, stand on a plate, remove the foil top, and replace with wax paper. Weigh down the top of the terrine with a can of food set on a small plate. Transfer to the refrigerator when cool enough and chill overnight.

Loosen the edge of the terrine with a knife, turn out, cut into thick slices, and serve.

carrot, orange & fennel soup

Preparation time **25 minutes**
Cooking temperature **low**
Cooking time **6¼–8¼ hours**
Serves **4**

2 tablespoons **butter**
1 tablespoon **sunflower oil**
1 large **onion**, chopped
1 teaspoon **fennel seeds**,
   roughly crushed
10 medium (1¼ lb) **carrots**,
   diced
grated rind and juice of
   1 **orange**
4¼ cups **vegetable stock**
salt and **black pepper**

To serve
½ cup **heavy cream**
handful of **croutons**

Preheat the slow cooker, if necessary; see the manufacturer's instructions. Heat the butter and oil in a skillet, add the onion, and fry, stirring, for 5 minutes or until the onion is just beginning to soften.

Stir in the fennel seeds and cook for 1 minute to release the flavor. Mix in the carrots, fry for an additional 2 minutes, then stir in the orange rind and juice. Turn into the slow cooker pot. Bring the stock to the boil in the skillet, add salt and black pepper, then pour into the slow cooker pot. Cover with the lid and cook on low for 6–8 hours or until the carrots are tender.

Transfer to a blender and puree, in batches if necessary, until smooth, then return to the slow cooker pot. Alternatively, puree the soup still in the slow cooker pot with an immersion hand blender. Reheat, if necessary, in the covered slow cooker pot for 15 minutes.

Ladle the soup into bowls and serve with drizzled cream and croutons.

For Moroccan-spiced carrot soup, prepare the soup as above, replacing the fennel seeds with 1 teaspoon cumin seeds and 1 teaspoon coriander seeds, both crushed, and ½ teaspoon of smoked paprika and ½ teaspoon of turmeric. Omit the orange rind and juice and add ⅔ cup milk or milk and heavy cream mixed before reheating.

meat, poultry, & game

lamb shanks with juniper

Preparation time **15 minutes**
Cooking temperature **high**
Cooking time **5–7 hours**
Serves **4**

2 tablespoons **butter**
4 **lamb shanks**, about 3 lb
   in total
2 small **red onions**, cut into
   wedges
2 tablespoons **all-purpose
   flour**
scant 1 cup **red wine**
scant 2 cups **lamb stock**
2 tablespoons **cranberry
   sauce** (optional)
1 tablespoon **tomato paste**
2 **bay leaves**
1 teaspoon **juniper berries**,
   roughly crushed
1 small **cinnamon stick**,
   halved
pared rind of 1 small **orange**
salt and **black pepper**

To serve
mashed **sweet potatoes**
green beans

Preheat the slow cooker, if necessary; see the
manufacturer's instructions. Heat the butter in a skillet,
add the lamb shanks, and fry over a medium heat,
turning until browned all over. Drain and put into the
slow cooker pot.

Add the onions to the skillet and fry for 4–5 minutes
or until just beginning to turn golden. Stir in the flour.
Gradually mix in the wine and stock, then add the
cranberry sauce (if used) and the remaining
ingredients. Bring to a boil, stirring.

Transfer to the slow cooker pot, cover with the lid,
and cook on high for 5–7 hours or until the lamb is
beginning to fall off the bone. If you prefer a thick
sauce, pour it into a saucepan and boil rapidly for
5 minutes or until reduced by one-third. Serve the lamb
with mashed sweet potatoes and green beans.

For lamb shanks with lemon, fry the lamb shanks
as above, then fry 2 sliced white onions. Mix with
the flour and add scant 1 cup dry white wine, the
lamb stock, 4 teaspoons roughly crushed coriander
seeds, the bay leaves, the pared rind of 1 lemon, and
2 teaspoons honey. Season and bring to a boil, pour
over the lamb, and cook as above.

thai green chicken curry

Preparation time **20 minutes**
Cooking temperature **low** and
high
Cooking time 8¼–10¼ **hours**
Serves **4**

1 tablespoon **sunflower oil**
2 tablespoons **Thai green
curry paste**
2 teaspoons **galangal paste**
2 Thai **green chilies**, seeded
and thinly sliced
1 **onion**, finely chopped
8 **chicken thighs**, about 2 lb
in total, skinned, boned and
cubed
1⅔ cups **coconut milk**
⅔ cup **chicken stock**
4 dried **kaffir lime leaves**
2 teaspoons **light brown
sugar**
2 teaspoons **Thai fish sauce**
3½ oz **sugar snap peas**
1 cup halved **green beans**
small bunch of **cilantro**

Preheat the slow cooker, if necessary; see the
manufacturer's instructions. Heat the oil in a skillet, add
the curry paste, galangal paste, and green chilies and
cook for 1 minute.

Stir in the onion and chicken and cook, stirring, until
the chicken is just beginning to turn golden. Pour in the
coconut milk and stock, then add the lime leaves, sugar,
and fish sauce. Bring to a boil, stirring.

Transfer the mixture into the slow cooker pot, cover
with the lid, and cook on low for 8–10 hours or until the
chicken is tender.

Stir in the peas and beans and cook on high for
15 minutes or until they are just tender. Tear the
cilantro leaves over the top, then spoon into bowls
and serve with rice.

For Thai red chicken curry, make up the curry as
above but omit the green curry paste and green
chilies and instead add 2 tablespoons red curry paste
and 2 finely chopped garlic cloves. Cook for 8–10
hours as above but do not add the peas and beans,
then spoon into bowls and sprinkle with some torn
cilantro leaves.

pork, orange & star anise

Preparation time **20 minutes**
Cooking temperature **low**
Cooking time **8–10 hours**
Serves **4**

1 tablespoon **sunflower oil**
4 **pork shoulder steaks** or
  boneless **sparerib chop**,
  about 1 lb 7 oz in total,
  each cut into 3
1 **onion**, chopped
2 tablespoons **all-purpose
  flour**
2 cups **chicken stock**
grated rind and juice of
  1 **orange**
3 tablespoons **plum sauce**
2 tablespoons **soy sauce**
3–4 whole **star anise**
1 fresh or dried **red chili**,
  halved (optional)
salt and **black pepper**
grated rind of **1 orange**
mashed **potatoes** mixed with
  steamed **green vegetables**,
  to serve

Preheat the slow cooker, if necessary; see the manufacturer's instructions. Heat the oil in a large skillet, add the pieces of pork, and fry over a high heat until browned on both sides. Lift the pork out of the pan with a slotted spoon and transfer to a plate.

Add the onion to the skillet and fry, stirring, for 5 minutes or until lightly browned. Stir in the flour, then mix in the stock, orange rind and juice, plum sauce, soy sauce, star anise, and chili (if used). Season with salt and black pepper, and bring to a boil, stirring.

Transfer the pork to the slow cooker pot and pour the sauce over it. Cover with the lid and cook on low for 8–10 hours. Sprinkle with grated orange rind and serve with mashed potatoes mixed with steamed green vegetables.

For pork, orange & bay leaves, prepare the dish as above, but replace the plum sauce, soy sauce, star anise, and red chili with 2 bay leaves, 2 teaspoons light brown sugar and 1 tablespoon balsamic vinegar.

creamy tarragon chicken

Preparation time **15 minutes**
Cooking temperature **high**
Cooking time **3–4 hours**
Serves **4**

1 tablespoon **olive oil**
1 tablespoon **butter**
4 boneless, skinless **chicken breasts**, about 1 lb in total
7 oz **shallots**, halved
1 tablespoon **all-purpose flour**
1 ¼ cups **chicken stock**
¼ cup **dry vermouth**
2 sprigs of **tarragon**, plus extra to serve
3 tablespoons **heavy cream**
2 tablespoons chopped **chives**
salt and **black pepper**
coarsely mashed **potatoes** mixed with **peas**, to serve

Preheat the slow cooker, if necessary; see the manufacturer's instructions. Heat the oil and butter in a skillet, add the chicken, and fry over a high heat until golden on both sides but not cooked through. Drain and put into the slow cooker pot in a single layer.

Add the shallots to the skillet and cook, stirring, for 4–5 minutes or until just beginning to turn golden. Stir in the flour, then gradually mix in the stock and vermouth. Add the sprigs of tarragon, a little salt and black pepper, and bring to the boil, stirring.

Pour the sauce over the chicken breasts, cover with the lid, and cook on high for 3–4 hours or until the chicken is cooked through to the center.

Stir the cream into the sauce and sprinkle the chicken with 1 tablespoon chopped tarragon and the chives. Serve with coarsely mashed potatoes mixed with peas.

For creamy pesto chicken, prepare the dish as above, but replace the vermouth with ¼ cup white wine and the tarragon with 1 tablespoon pesto. Sprinkle the chicken with some tiny basil leaves and a little grated Parmesan cheese instead of the chives. Serve the chicken sliced, if liked, and mixed with cooked penne pasta and drizzled with the creamy sauce.

beef chili with cheesy tortillas

Preparation time **20 minutes**
Cooking temperature **low**
Cooking time **8–10 hours**
Serves **4**

1 tablespoon **sunflower oil**
1 lb extra lean **ground beef**
1 **onion**, chopped
2 **garlic cloves**, finely
   chopped
1 teaspoon **smoked paprika**
½ teaspoon crushed dried
   red chilies
1 teaspoon **ground cumin**
1 tablespoon **all-purpose
   flour**
13 oz canned **chopped
   tomatoes**
13½ oz canned **red kidney
   beans**, drained
⅔ cup **beef stock**
1 tablespoon **dark brown
   sugar**
salt and **black pepper**

Topping
3½ oz **tortilla chips**
½ **red bell pepper**, cored,
   seeded, and diced
chopped **cilantro**
1 cup shredded sharp
   cheddar cheese

Preheat the slow cooker, if necessary; see the
manufacturer's instructions. Heat the oil in a skillet,
add the meat and onion, and fry, stirring, for 5 minutes,
breaking up the meat with a spoon until it is browned.

Stir in the garlic, paprika, chilies, and cumin and cook
for 2 minutes. Stir in the flour. Mix in the tomatoes,
kidney beans, stock, and sugar, season with salt and
black pepper and pour the mixture into the slow cooker
pot. Cover with the lid and cook on low for 8–10 hours.

Stir the chili, then arrange the tortilla chips on top.
Sprinkle over the remaining ingredients, lift the pot
out of the housing using oven mitts and brown under
broiler until the cheese just melts. Spoon into bowls
to serve.

For turkey fajitas with guacamole, make up the chili
as above, using 1 lb ground turkey instead of the beef.
To serve, halve, pit, and peel 1 avocado and mash the
flesh with the juice of 1 lime, a small bunch of torn
fresh cilantro and some salt and black pepper. Spoon
the turkey mixture onto 8 warmed, medium soft flour
tortillas, top with spoonfuls of guacamole, and a
tablespoon each of sour cream, if liked, and roll
up to serve.

cidered pork with sage dumplings

Preparation time **25 minutes**
Cooking temperature **low**
Cooking time **9–11 hours**
Serves **4**

1 tablespoon **sunflower oil**
1½ lb **pork shoulder steaks**,
    cubed and any fat discarded
1 **leek**, thinly sliced, the
    green and white parts kept
    separate
2 tablespoons **all-purpose
    flour**
1¼ cups **dry hard cider**
1¼ cups **chicken stock**
4 medium **carrots**, diced
1 **apple**, cored and diced
2–3 stems of **sage**
salt and **black pepper**

Dumplings

1¼ cups **self-rising flour**
⅓ cup **vegetable shortening**
1 tablespoon chopped **sage**
2 tablespoons chopped
    parsley
5–7 tablespoons **water**

Preheat the slow cooker, if necessary; see the
manufacturer's instructions. Heat the oil in a skillet,
add the pork a few pieces at a time until all the pieces
are in the pan, then fry over a high heat until lightly
browned. Lift out of the skillet with a slotted spoon
and transfer to the slow cooker pot.

Add the white leek slices to the skillet and fry for
2–3 minutes or until softened. Stir in the flour, then
gradually mix in the cider and stock. Add the carrot,
apple, sage, and some salt and black pepper. Bring to a
boil, stirring. Pour the mixture into the slow cooker pot,
cover with the lid, and cook on low for 8–10 hours or
until the pork is tender.

Make the dumplings. Put the flour, shortening, herbs,
and a little salt and black pepper into a bowl, mix
together, then gradually stir in enough water to make
a soft but not sticky dough. Cut into 12 pieces and roll
into balls with floured hands. Stir the green leek slices
into the pork casserole and arrange the dumplings on
the top. Cover and cook, still on low, for 1 hour, until
they are well risen. Spoon into shallow bowls to serve.

For beery pork with rosemary dumplings, make
up the casserole as above, adding 1¼ cups blonde
beer or lager instead of the hard cider and 2¼ cups
mixed diced parsnip, carrot, and rutabaga instead
of the carrots, and apple. Flavor with 2 stems of
rosemary instead of the sage and add 1 tablespoon
chopped rosemary instead of sage to the dumplings.

kashmiri butter chicken

Preparation time **30 minutes**
Cooking temperature **low**
Cooking time **5–7 hours**
Serves **4**

2 **onions**, quartered
3 **garlic cloves**
1½ inch **fresh ginger**, peeled
1 large **red chili**, seeded
8 boneless, skinless **chicken
  thighs**
1 tablespoon **sunflower oil**
2 tablespoons **butter**
1 teaspoon **cumin seeds**,
  crushed
1 teaspoon **fennel seeds**,
  crushed
4 **cardamom pods**, crushed
1 teaspoon **paprika**
1 teaspoon **ground turmeric**
¼ teaspoon **ground cinnamon**
1¼ cups **chicken stock**
1 tablespoon **brown sugar**
2 tablespoons **tomato paste**
⅓ cup **heavy cream**
salt

To garnish
toasted slivered almonds
sprigs of **cilantro**

Preheat the slow cooker, if necessary; see the manufacturer's instructions. Blend the onions, garlic, ginger, and chili in a food processor or blender or chop finely.

Cut each chicken thigh into 4 pieces. Heat the oil in a large skillet and add the chicken a few pieces at a time until all the meat has been added. Cook over high heat until browned. Drain and transfer to a plate.

Add the butter to the skillet. When it has melted, add the onion paste and cook over a more moderate heat until it is just beginning to color. Stir in the cumin and fennel seeds, cardamom pods, and ground spices. Cook for 1 minute, then mix in the stock, sugar, tomato paste, and salt. Bring to a boil, stirring.

Transfer the chicken to the slow cooker pot, pour the onion mixture and sauce over the top, and press the pieces of chicken below the surface of the liquid. Cover with the lid and cook on low for 5–7 hours.

Stir in the cream. Garnish with toasted slivered almonds and sprigs of cilantro and serve with plain boiled rice.

For cilantro flat breads to accompany the curry, mix together 1⅔ cups self-rising flour, ½ teaspoon baking powder, 3 tablespoons roughly chopped cilantro leaves, and a little salt in a bowl. Add 2 tablespoons sunflower oil, then gradually mix in 6–7 tablespoons water to make a soft dough. Cut the dough into 4 pieces and roll out each piece thinly on a lightly floured surface to form a rough oval. Cook on a preheated, ridged grill pan for 3–4 minutes on each side, until singed and puffy.

red cooked chinese duck

Preparation time **20 minutes**
Cooking temperature **high**
Cooking time **5–6 hours**
Serves **4**

4 **duck legs**, each about
 7 oz
1 **onion**, sliced
2 tablespoons **all-purpose
 flour**
2 cups **chicken stock**
2 tablespoons **soy sauce**
1 tablespoon **red wine
 vinegar**
1 tablespoon **honey**
2 teaspoons **tomato paste**
2 teaspoons **Thai fish sauce**
½ teaspoon crushed dried
 red chilies
½ teaspoon **ground allspice**
4 **star anise**
5–6 **red plums**, pitted and
 quartered
rice or **gingered noodles**,
 to serve

Preheat the slow cooker, if necessary; see the manufacturer's instructions. Dry-fry the duck legs in a skillet over a low heat at first until the fat begins to run, then increase the heat and brown on both sides. Lift out of the skillet with a slotted spoon and transfer to the slow cooker pot.

Pour off all but 1 tablespoon of the duck fat from the pan, then add the onion and fry, stirring, for 5 minutes or until just turning golden. Stir in the flour, then gradually mix in the stock. Add the remaining ingredients, except for the plums, and bring to a boil, stirring.

Pour the sauce over the duck, add the plums, and press the duck beneath the surface of the liquid. Cover with the lid and cook on high for 5–6 hours or until the duck is almost falling off the bones. Serve with rice or with gingered noodles (see below).

For gingered noodles to accompany the duck, heat 1 tablespoon sesame oil in a wok, add 1 inch piece peeled and finely chopped fresh ginger, 2 cups finely bok choy, ½ cup halved snow peas, and 3 packages, each 5 oz, of thick-cut, straight-to-wok noodles. Stir-fry for 3–4 minutes or until the bok choy has just wilted and the noodles are hot.

baked ham in cola

Preparation time **15 minutes**
Cooking temperature **high**
Cooking time **6–7 hours**
Serves **4**

2½ lb boneless **smoked ham**,
   soaked overnight in cold
   water
5 **cloves**
1 **onion**, cut into 8 wedges
2 **carrots**, thickly sliced
13½ oz canned **black beans**
   or **red kidney beans**,
   drained
2 **bay leaves**
3¾ cups **cola**
1 tablespoon **dark brown
   sugar**
1 tablespoon **tomato paste**
2 teaspoons **English mustard**

Preheat the slow cooker, if necessary; see the manufacturer's instructions. Drain the ham and put it into the slow cooker pot. Press the cloves into 5 of the onion wedges and add with the remaining onion wedges and carrot slices to the ham. Add the drained beans and add the bay leaves.

Pour the cola into a saucepan, add the sugar, tomato paste, and mustard and bring to a boil, stirring. Pour over the ham, cover with the lid, and cook on high for 6–7 hours or until the ham is tender.

Strain the cooking liquid into a saucepan and boil rapidly for 10 minutes to reduce by half. Keep the ham and vegetables hot in the turned-off slow cooker with the lid on.

Slice the ham thinly and arrange on plates with the vegetables, beans, and a drizzle of sauce. Serve with baked potatoes and broccoli, if liked.

For baked ham with parsley sauce, soak the ham as above and cook in the slow cooker pot with the cloves, onion, carrots, bay leaves, and 3¾ cups boiling water instead of the cola. Omit the beans and remaining ingredients. Melt 2 tablespoons butter in a saucepan for the parsley sauce. Stir in 3 tablespoons all-purpose, cook for 1 minute, then mix in 1¼ cups milk. Bring to a boil, stirring until thickened and smooth. Stir in 1 teaspoon English mustard, 3 tablespoons chopped parsley, and salt and black pepper. Serve with the sliced ham and drained onion and carrots.

lamb rogan josh

Preparation time **15 minutes**
Cooking temperature **low**
Cooking time **8–10 hours**
Serves **4**

2 tablespoons **butter**
1½ lb **lamb fillet**, sliced
2 **onions**, chopped
3 **garlic cloves**, finely
  chopped
1 inch **fresh ginger**, peeled
  and finely chopped
1 teaspoon **ground turmeric**
2 teaspoons **ground
  coriander**
2 teaspoons **cumin seeds**,
  roughly crushed
2 teaspoons **garam masala**
½ teaspoon crushed dried
  red chilies
2 tablespoons **all-purpose
  flour**
13 oz canned **chopped
  tomatoes**
1¼ cups **lamb stock**
¼ cup **heavy cream**

To garnish
small bunch of **cilantro**, leaves
  torn
shredded **red onion**

Preheat the slow cooker, if necessary; see the manufacturer's instructions. Heat the butter in a skillet, add the lamb a few pieces at a time until all the meat is in the skillet, then fry, stirring, over a high heat until browned. Lift out of the skillet with a slotted spoon and add to the slow cooker pot.

Add the onions to the skillet and fry, stirring, for 5 minutes or until softened and just beginning to turn golden. Stir in the garlic, ginger, spices, and dried chilies and cook for 1 minute. Mix in the flour, then add the tomatoes and stock. Bring to a boil, stirring.

Pour the tomato mixture over the lamb, cover with the lid, and cook on low for 8–10 hours or until the lamb is tender. Stir in the cream, garnish with cilantro leaves and serve with pilaf rice (see below) and naan, if liked.

For pilaf rice to accompany the curry, rinse 1¼ cups basmati rice in a strainer several times, drain, then soak in cold water for 15 minutes. Heat 1 tablespoon butter in a saucepan, add 1 finely chopped onion, and fry for 3 minutes. Add 5 lightly crushed cardamom pods, 5 cloves, ½ cinnamon stick, ½ teaspoon ground turmeric, and ½ teaspoon salt. Cook for 1 minute. Drain the rice, add to the pan, and cook for 1 minute. Pour in 2 cups boiling water, bring back to a boil, cover tightly, and simmer gently for 10 minutes. Take the saucepan from the heat but do not remove the lid. Let stand for 8–10 minutes. Fluff up with a fork and serve.

beef stew with dumplings

Preparation time **35 minutes**

Cooking temperature **low** and **high**

Cooking time **8–10½ hours**

Serves **4**

2 tablespoons **olive oil**

1½ lb **braising beef**, cubed and any fat discarded

1 large **onion**, chopped

2–3 **garlic cloves**, chopped

2 tablespoons **all-purpose flour**

1¼ cups Burgundy **red wine**

1¼ cups **beef stock**

1 tablespoon **tomato paste**

2 **bay leaves**

150 g (5 oz) baby **carrots**, larger ones halved

1⅓ cups trimmed, cleaned, and thinly sliced **leeks**

salt and **black pepper**

Horseradish dumplings

1¼ cups **self-rising flour**

⅓ cup **lard**

2 teaspoons **creamed horseradish**

3 tablespoons snipped **chives**

5–7 tablespoons **water**

salt and **black pepper**

Preheat the slow cooker, if necessary; see the manufacturer's instructions. Heat the oil in a skillet and add the beef, a few cubes at a time, until all the pieces have been added to the skillet. Fry over high heat until just beginning to brown, then add the onion and fry, stirring, for 5 minutes.

Stir in the garlic and flour, then gradually mix in the wine and stock. Add the tomato paste and bay leaves and season with salt and black pepper. Bring to a boil, then transfer the mixture to the slow cooker pot. Cover with the lid and cook on low for 7–9 hours.

Stir the stew, then add the carrots, replace the lid, and cook on high for 30–45 minutes.

Meanwhile, make the dumplings. Mix the flour, lard, horseradish, chives, and salt and black pepper in a bowl. Stir in enough water to make a soft but not sticky dough. With floured hands, shape into 8 balls.

Stir the leeks into the stew, then add the dumplings, replace the lid, and cook for another 30–45 minutes still on high or until the dumplings are light and fluffy. Spoon into shallow dishes and serve, remembering to remove the bay leaves.

For Guinness beef stew with mustard dumplings,

make up the stew as above, replacing the red wine with 1¼ cups Guinness or stout. Top with dumplings made with 3 teaspoons whole-grain mustard instead of the creamed horeradish and chives.

slow-braised pork with ratatouille

Preparation time **20 minutes**
Cooking temperature **high**
Cooking time **7–9 hours**
Serves **4**

1 tablespoon **olive oil**
1 **onion**, chopped
1 **red bell pepper**, cored, seeded, and cut into chunks
1 **yellow bell pepper**, cored, seeded, and cut into chunks
2 medium **zucchini**, cut into chunks
2 **garlic cloves**, finely chopped
13 oz canned **chopped tomatoes**
⅔ cup **red wine** or **chicken stock**
1 tablespoon **cornstarch**
2–3 stems of **rosemary**, leaves torn from stems
1¾ lb piece thick end **pork belly**, rind and any twine removed
salt and **black pepper**
mashed **potatoes**, to serve

Preheat the slow cooker, if necessary; see the manufacturer's instructions. Heat the oil in a skillet, add the onion, and fry, stirring, for 5 minutes or until just beginning to turn golden.

Add the black peppers, zucchini, and garlic and fry for 2 minutes, then mix in the tomatoes and the wine or stock. Mix the cornstarch to a smooth paste with a little water, then stir into the skillet with the rosemary leaves and some seasoning. Bring to a boil, stirring.

Turn half the mixture into the slow cooker pot, add the unrolled pork belly and cover with the rest of the vegetable mixture. Cover with the lid and cook on high for 7–9 hours or until the pork is almost falling apart. If you like your sauces thick, ladle it out of the slow cooker pot into a saucepan and boil for 5 minutes to reduce down. Cut the pork into 4 pieces, then spoon into shallow dishes and serve with mashed potatoes and the tomato sauce.

For braised chicken with ratatouille, fry 4 chicken thigh and leg joints in 1 tablespoon olive oil until browned on both sides. Drain and transfer to the slow cooker pot. Make up the ratatouille as above, spoon it over the chicken, and cook on high for 5–6 hours.

sun-dried tomato & chicken pilaf

Preparation time **25 minutes**
Cooking temperature **high**
Cooking time **3–4 hours**
Serves **4**

1 tablespoon **olive oil**
4 boneless, skinless **chicken breasts**
1 large **onion**, roughly chopped
2 **garlic cloves**, chopped (optional)
13 oz canned **chopped tomatoes**
½ cup drained **sun-dried tomatoes** in oil, sliced
2 teaspoons **pesto**
2½ cups hot **chicken stock**
¾ cup **instant brown rice**
¼ cup **wild rice**
salt and **black pepper**

To serve
arugula salad
olive oil and **lemon** dressing

Preheat the slow cooker, if necessary; see the manufacturer's instructions. Heat the oil in a skillet and fry the chicken breasts on only one side until browned. Remove from the skillet with a slotted spoon and reserve on a plate.

Fry the onion and garlic (if used) in the skillet, stirring, for 5 minutes or until lightly browned. Add the tomatoes, sun-dried tomatoes, and pesto, season with salt and black pepper and bring to a boil. Pour into the slow cooker pot, then stir in the stock.

Rinse the brown rice well in a strainer under cold running water, then stir into the slow cooker pot with the wild rice. Arrange the chicken breasts on top of the rice, browned side up, pressing them just below the level of the liquid so that they don't dry out during cooking. Cover with the lid and cook on high for 3–4 hours or until the chicken is cooked and the rice is tender.

Spoon onto serving plates and serve with an arugula salad tossed in an olive oil and lemon dressing

For red bell pepper, lemon & chicken pilaf, fry 4 boneless, skinless chicken breasts as above and transfer to a plate. In the skillet, fry 1 large, roughly chopped onion and 1 cored, seeded, and diced red bell pepper until the onion is just turning golden. Add 13 oz canned chopped tomatoes and 2 tablespoons finely chopped lemon thyme leaves and the grated rind and juice of 1 lemon. Bring to a boil, add to the slow cooker with 2½ cups hot chicken stock, ¾ cups instant brown rice, and the chicken. Continue as above.

moussaka

Preparation time **30 minutes**
Cooking temperature **low**
Cooking time **8¾–11¼ hours**
Serves **4**

¼ cup **olive oil**
1 large **eggplant**, thinly sliced
1 lb **ground lamb**
1 **onion**, chopped
2 **garlic cloves**, finely
  chopped
1 tablespoon **all-purpose
  flour**
13 oz canned **chopped
  tomatoes**
1 cup **lamb stock**
1 teaspoon **ground cinnamon**
¼ teaspoon grated **nutmeg**
1 tablespoon **tomato paste**
salt and **black pepper**

Topping
3 **eggs**
1 cup **plain yogurt**
3 oz crumbled **feta cheese**
pinch of grated **nutmeg**

Preheat the slow cooker, if necessary; see the manufacturer's instructions. Heat half the oil in a skillet and fry the eggplant slices in batches, adding more oil as needed, until they have all been fried and are softened and lightly browned on both sides. Drain and transfer to a plate.

Add the ground lamb and onion to the skillet and dry-fry, stirring and breaking up the lamb, until evenly browned. Stir in the garlic and flour, then mix in the tomatoes, stock, spices, tomato paste and a little salt and black pepper. Bring to a boil, stirring.

Spoon the lamb mixture into the slow cooker pot and arrange the eggplant slices on top, overlapping. Cover with the lid and cook on low for 8–10 hours.

Make the custard topping. Mix together the eggs, yogurt, feta, nutmeg, and spoon over the top of the eggplant. Replace the lid and cook, still on low, for ¾–1¼ hours or until set. Lift the pot out of the housing using oven mitts and brown under a hot broiler. Serve with salad.

For Greek shepherds' pie, prepare the ground meat, top with the fried eggplant slices, and cook as above. Omit the custard topping and instead peel and cut medium potatoes into chunks and cook in a saucepan of boiling water for 15 minutes or until soft. Drain and mash with 3 tablespoons Greek yogurt and some salt and black pepper. Lift the pot out of the housing, spoon the mash over the eggplant, dot with 2 tablespoons butter, and brown under a hot grill.

sausages with onion gravy

Preparation time **15 minutes**
Cooking temperature **low**
Cooking time **6–8 hours**
Serves **4**

1 tablespoon **sunflower oil**
8 "gourmet" flavored
  sausages, such as **Sicilian**
  or **Toulouse**
2 **red onions**, halved and
  thinly sliced
2 teaspoons **light brown**
  sugar
2 tablespoons **all-purpose**
  flour
2 cups **beef stock**
1 tablespoons sun-dried or
  ordinary **tomato paste**
1 **bay leaf**
salt and **black pepper**

To serve
large **Yorkshire puddings**
steamed **carrots**
steamed **broccoli**

Preheat the slow cooker, if necessary; see the manufacturer's instructions. Heat the oil in a skillet, add the sausages, and fry over a high heat for 5 minutes, turning until browned on all sides but not cooked through. Drain and transfer to the slow cooker pot.

Add the onions to the skillet and fry over a medium heat for 5 minutes or until softened. Add the sugar and fry, stirring, for 5 more minutes or until the onion slices are caramelized around the edges.

Stir in the flour, then gradually mix in the stock. Add the tomato paste, the bay leaf, and some salt and black pepper and bring to a boil, still stirring. Pour over the sausages. Cover with the lid and cook on low for 6–8 hours or until the sausages are tender.

Serve spooned into large Yorkshire puddings, prepared from a Yorkshire pudding mix (available at specialty British food stores), accompanied with steamed carrots and broccoli or mashed potatoes.

For sausages with beery onion gravy, fry 8 large traditional herb sausages instead of the "gourmet" ones until browned. Drain, then fry 2 sliced white onions until softened, and omit the sugar. Stir in all-purpose flour, then mix in ⅔ cup stout or brown beer and reduce the beef stock to 1¼ cups. Replace the tomato paste with 1 tablespoon whole-grain mustard and 2 tablespoons Worcestershire sauce. Season and bring to a boil. Cook in the slow cooker for 6–8 hours.

pheasant with pancetta

Preparation time **35 minutes**
Cooking temperature **low**
Cooking time **2½–3 hours**
Serves **4**

4 **pheasant breasts**, about
  1 lb 3 oz in total
small bunch of **sage**
3½ oz **smoked pancetta**,
  sliced
2 tablespoons **butter**
7 oz **shallots**, halved if large
2 tablespoons **all-purpose**
  flour
⅔ cup **dry hard cider**
⅔ cup **chicken stock**
1 teaspoon **Dijon mustard**
1 **apple**, cored and sliced
7¾ oz canned whole peeled
  chestnuts, drained
salt and **black pepper**
steamed **baby carrots**,
  to serve

Preheat the slow cooker, if necessary; see the
manufacturer's instructions. Rinse the pheasant breasts
with cold water, pat dry with paper towels, and season
well with salt and black pepper. Top each breast with
a few sage leaves, then wrap in pancetta slices until
completely covered. Tie at intervals with fine kitchen
twine to keep the pancetta in place.

Heat the butter in a skillet, add the shallots, and fry
for 4–5 minutes or until browned. Stir in the flour, then
add the cider, stock, and mustard. Add the apple and
chestnuts and a little extra salt and black pepper.
Bring to a boil, stirring.

Arrange the pheasant breasts in the slow cooker
pot. Pour the hot onion mixture over the top, cover
with the lid, and cook on low for 2½–3 hours or until
the pheasant is tender and cooked through to the
center. Spoon onto plates, remove the twine from
the pheasant, and serve with baby carrots.

For pheasant with bacon & red wine, add a sage
leaf to each pheasant breast, then wrap each one with
a stretched slice of smoked fatty bacon. Fry as above
with the shallots until the bacon is browned. Stir in the
flour, then add 1¼ cups red wine in place of the cider,
stock, and mustard. Omit the apple and instead add
8 halved dried plums (prunes) and the chestnuts.
Cook as above.

sweet & sour chicken

Preparation time **20 minutes**
Cooking temperature **low**
Cooking time **6¼–8¼ hours**
Serves **4**

1 tablespoon **sunflower oil**
8 small **chicken thighs**, about
  2 lb in total, skinned, boned,
  and cubed
4 **scallions**, thickly sliced;
  white and green parts kept
  separate
2 **carrots**, halved lengthwise
  and thinly sliced
1 inch **fresh ginger**, peeled
  and finely chopped
14¼ oz can **pineapple chunks**
  in natural juice
1¼ cups **chicken stock**
1 tablespoon **cornstarch**
1 tablespoon **tomato paste**
2 tablespoons **superfine
  sugar**
2 tablespoons **soy sauce**
2 tablespoons **malt vinegar**
½ oz canned **bamboo shoots**,
  drained
1⅛ cups **bean sprouts**
1 cup thinly sliced **snow peas**
rice, to serve

Preheat the slow cooker, if necessary; see the manufacturer's instructions. Heat the oil in a skillet, add the chicken thighs, and fry, stirring, until browned on all sides. Mix in the white sliced scallions, carrots, and ginger and cook for 2 minutes.

Stir in the pineapple chunks and their juice and the stock. Put the cornstarch, tomato paste, and sugar into a small bowl, then gradually mix in the soy sauce and vinegar to make a smooth paste. Stir into the skillet and bring to a boil, stirring.

Turn the chicken and sauce into the slow cooker pot, add the bamboo shoots, and press the chicken beneath the surface of the sauce. Cover with the lid and cook on low for 6–8 hours.

When almost ready to serve, add the green scallions, the bean sprouts, and snow peas to the slow cooker pot and mix well. Replace the lid and cook, still on low, for 15 minutes or until the vegetables are just tender. Spoon into rice-filled bowls.

For lemon chicken, make up the recipe as above to the addition of the chicken stock. Gradually mix the juice of 1 lemon into the cornstarch to make a smooth paste, then stir into the stock with 2 tablespoons dry sherry and 4 teaspoons superfine sugar. Bring to a boil, stirring, then add to the slow cooker pot and cook as above, adding the green scallions, bean sprouts, and snow peas at the end.

spiced meatballs with dill sauce

Preparation time **25 minutes**
Cooking temperature **low**
Cooking time **6–8 hours**
Serves **4**

1 **onion**, quartered
2 slices **bread**
8 oz ground **pork**
8 oz ground **beef**
1 teaspoon **ground allspice**
1 **egg yolk**
1 tablespoon **sunflower oil**
salt and **black pepper**
mashed **potato**, to serve

Sauce
1 tablespoon **butter**
1 **onion**, sliced
2 tablespoons **all-purpose flour**
2½ cups **chicken stock**
4 teaspoons chopped **dill**, plus extra to garnish

Preheat the slow cooker, if necessary; see the manufacturer's instructions. Finely chop the onion and bread in a food processor or blender. Add the ground meats, allspice, egg yolk, and a little seasoning and mix together.

Divide the meat mixture into 24 and roll into balls with wetted hands. Heat the oil in a skillet, add the meatballs, and fry over a medium heat, turning until evenly browned but not cooked through. Drain and transfer to the slow cooker pot.

Make the sauce. Add the butter and onion to the cleaned skillet. Fry, stirring, for 5 minutes or until the onion is softened and just beginning to turn golden. Stir in the flour, then gradually mix in the stock and bring to a boil, stirring. Season and pour the sauce over the meatballs. Cover with the lid and cook on low for 6–8 hours.

Stir the chopped dill into the sauce and serve the meatballs with mashed potato sprinkled with a little extra chopped dill to garnish.

For meatballs in tomato sauce, make up the meatballs as above but omit the allspice. For the sauce, fry 1 chopped onion in 1 tablespoon olive oil. Add 2 finely chopped garlic cloves, 13 oz canned chopped tomatoes, 1 teaspoon superfine sugar, ⅔ cup chicken stock, and salt and black pepper. Bring to a boil, pour over the meatballs and cook as above. Finish with some torn basil leaves and serve with pasta.

peppered venison with biscuits

Preparation time **35 minutes**
Cooking temperature **low** and
   high
Cooking time **8¾–11 hours**
Serves **4**

2 tablespoons **butter**
1 tablespoon **olive oil**
1½ lb **venison shoulder**, diced
1 large **red onion**, sliced
1¾ cups sliced **cup
   mushrooms**
2 **garlic cloves**, chopped
2 tablespoons **all-purpose
   flour**
scant 1 cup **red wine**
1 cup **chicken stock**
2 teaspoons **tomato paste**
2 tablespoons **red-currant
   jelly**
1 teaspoon crushed **black
   peppercorns**
salt

Biscuits
2 cups **self-rising flour**
3 tablespoons **butter**, diced
4 oz **Gorgonzola cheese**
3 tablespoons chopped
   parsley or **chives**
1 **egg**, beaten
4–5 tablespoons **milk**

Preheat the slow cooker, if necessary; see the
manufacturer's instructions. Heat the butter and oil
in a large skillet, add the diced venison a few pieces
at time until all the meat has been added, then fry until
evenly browned. Transfer to a plate.

Add the onion to the skillet and fry for 5 minutes.
Stir in the mushrooms, garlic, and flour and cook for
1 minute. Stir in the wine, stock, tomato paste, red-
currant jelly, black peppercorns, and salt and bring
to a boil.

Arrange the venison in the slow cooker pot, add
the hot wine mixture, and press the venison below
the surface. Cover with the lid and cook on low for
8–10 hours.

When almost ready to serve, make the biscuits. Put
the flour in a bowl, add the butter, and rub in with
the fingertips until the mixture resembles fine bread
crumbs. Stir in a little salt and black pepper, the cheese
and herbs. Reserve 1 tablespoon of egg for glazing
and add the rest. Gradually mix in enough milk to
make a soft dough.

Knead lightly, then pat the dough into a thick oval or
a round that is a little smaller than the top of your slow
cooker. Cut it into 8 wedges and arrange, spaced
slightly apart, on top of the venison. Cover and cook
on high for ¾–1 hour.

Lift the pot out of the housing using oven mitts, brush
the biscuits with the reserved egg, and brown under
the broiler. Serve with green beans, if liked.

maple-glazed ribs

Preparation time **25 minutes**
Cooking temperature **high**
Cooking time **5–7 hours**
Serves **4**

2½ lb **pork ribs**, rinsed with
  cold water and drained
1 **onion**, quartered
1 **carrot**, thickly sliced
2 **bay leaves**
2 tablespoons **malt vinegar**
1 teaspoon **black black**
  peppercorns
½ teaspoon **salt**
4¼ cups boiling **water**

Glaze

2 teaspoons **English mustard**
1 teaspoon **ground allspice**
2 tablespoons **tomato paste**
2 tablespoons **brown sugar**
½ cup **maple syrup**

Coleslaw

2 **carrots**, grated
¼ **red cabbage**, shredded
3 **scallions**, sliced
½ cup **corn kernels**, thawed
  if frozen
2 tablespoons **mayonnaise**
2 tablespoons **plain yogurt**

Preheat the slow cooker, if necessary; see the manufacturer's instructions. Put the pork, onion, carrot, bay leaves, vinegar, black peppercorns, salt, and water into the slow cooker pot, cover with the lid, and cook on high for 5–7 hours or until the ribs are tender.

Lift the ribs out of the slow cooker using a slotted spoon and transfer to a foil-lined broiler pan. Mix together the ingredients for the glaze with ⅔ cup hot stock from the slow cooker pot. Spoon over the ribs, then broil them for 10–15 minutes, turning once or twice, until browned and sticky.

Meanwhile, mix the ingredients for the coleslaw together and spoon into 4 small bowls. Place these on dinner plates, then pile the ribs onto the plates to serve.

For Chinese ribs, cook the pork ribs in the slow cooker as above. Drain and transfer to a foil-lined broiler pan, then glaze with a mixture of 2 tablespoons tomato paste, 2 tablespoons soy sauce, ½ cup hoisin sauce, 2 tablespoons light muscovado sugar, the juice of 1 orange, and ⅔ cup stock from the slow cooker pot. Broil for 10–15 minutes as above.

gourmet bolognese

Preparation time **20 minutes**
Cooking temperature **low**
Cooking time **8–10 hours**
Serves **4**

1 tablespoon **olive oil**
1 lb lean **ground beef**
1 **onion**, chopped
7½ oz **chicken livers**, thawed
   if frozen
2 **garlic cloves**, finely
   chopped
2 oz **pancetta** or **smoked
   lean bacon**, diced
2 cups sliced **cup
   mushrooms**,
1 tablespoon **all-purpose
   flour**
⅔ cup **red wine**
⅔ cup **beef stock**
13 oz canned **chopped
   tomatoes**
2 tablespoons **tomato paste**
1 **bouquet garni**
salt and **black pepper**
10 oz **tagliatelle**

To serve
shaved **Parmesan cheese**
basil leaves

Preheat the slow cooker, if necessary; see the
manufacturer's instructions. Heat the oil in a skillet,
add the ground beef and onion, and fry, stirring
and breaking up the meat with a spoon until it is
evenly browned.

Meanwhile, rinse the chicken livers in a strainer, drain,
and then chop roughly, discarding any white cores.
Add to the skillet with the garlic, pancetta or bacon,
and mushrooms and cook for 2–3 minutes or until
the livers are browned.

Stir in the flour, then mix in the wine, stock, tomatoes,
tomato paste, bouquet garni, and seasoning. Bring to
a boil, stirring. Spoon into the slow cooker pot, cover
with the lid, and cook on low for 8–10 hours.

Just before serving, add the tagliatelle to a saucepan
of boiling salted water and cook for 8 minutes or until
just tender. Drain and stir into the bolognese. Spoon
into shallow bowls and sprinkle with Parmesan
shavings and some basil leaves.

For budget bolognese, omit the chicken livers
and pancetta or bacon and add 1 diced carrot and
1 diced zucchini along with the garlic and mushrooms.
Replace the wine with extra stock and continue
as above.

chicken pot-roast with lemon

Preparation time **25 minutes**
Cooking temperature **high**
Cooking time **5–6 hours**
Serves **4–5**

3 lb whole **chicken**
2 tablespoons **olive oil**
1 large **onion**, cut into
  6 wedges
2 cups **dry hard cider**
3 teaspoons **Dijon mustard**
2 teaspoons **superfine sugar**
3¾ cups hot **chicken stock**
3 **carrots**, cut into chunks
3 **celery ribs**, thickly sliced
1 **lemon**, cut into 6 wedges
½ cup **tarragon**
3 tablespoons **crème fraîche**
  (or 1½ tablespoons
  whipping cream mixed with
  1½ tablespoons sour cream)
salt and **black pepper**

Preheat the slow cooker, if necessary; see the manufacturer's instructions. Wash the chicken inside and out with cold water and pat dry with paper towels. Heat the oil in a large skillet, add the chicken, breast side down, and fry for 10 minutes, turning the chicken several times until browned all over.

Put the chicken, breast side down, in the slow cooker pot. Fry the onion wedges in the remaining oil in the skillet until lightly browned. Add the cider, mustard, and sugar and season with salt and black pepper. Bring to a boil, then pour over the chicken. Add the hot stock, then the vegetables, lemon wedges, and 3 sprigs of the tarragon, making sure that the chicken and all the vegetables are well below the level of the stock so that they cook evenly and thoroughly.

Cover with the lid and cook on high for 5–6 hours or until the chicken is thoroughly cooked and the meat juices run clear when the thickest parts of the leg and breast are pierced with a sharp knife. Turn the chicken after 4 hours, if liked.

Lift the chicken out of the stock, drain well, and transfer to a large serving plate. Remove the vegetables with a slotted spoon and arrange them around the chicken. Measure 2½ cups of the hot cooking stock from the slow cooker pot into a pitcher. Reserve a few sprigs of tarragon to garnish, chop the remainder, and whisk into the pitcher with the crème fraîche to make a gravy. Adjust the seasoning to taste. Carve the chicken in the usual way and serve with the gravy and vegetables. Garnish with lemon wedges, if liked, and the reserved tarragon sprigs, torn into pieces.

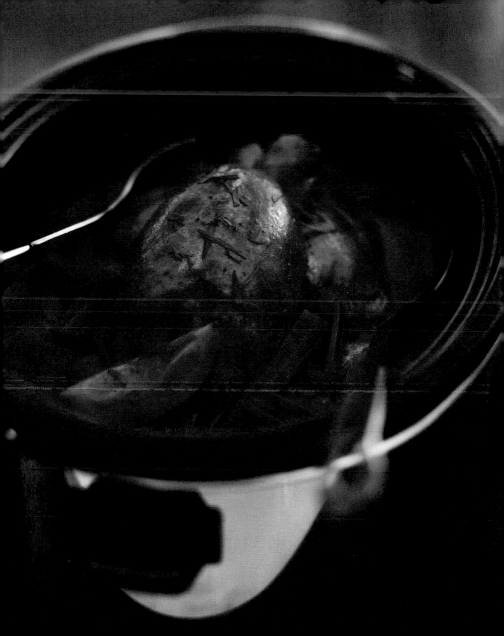

beef & root vegetable hotchpotch

Preparation time **25 minutes**
Cooking temperature **high**
Cooking time **7–8 hours**
Serves **4**

1 tablespoon **sunflower oil**
1½ lb **braising beef**, cubed
1 **onion**, chopped
2 tablespoons **all-purpose
  flour**
2½ cups **beef stock**
2 tablespoons **Worcestershire
  sauce**
1 tablespoon **tomato paste**
2 teaspoons **English mustard**
3 sprigs of **rosemary**
1 cup diced **carrots**
1 cup diced **rutabaga**
1 cup diced **parsnip**
6 medium (1 lb 6 oz)
  potatoes, thinly sliced
2 tablespoons **butter**
salt and **black pepper**

Preheat the slow cooker, if necessary; see the manufacturer's instructions. Heat the oil in a skillet, add the beef a few pieces at a time until all the meat is in the pan, then fry over a high heat, stirring, until browned. Scoop the beef out of skillet with a slotted spoon and transfer to the slow cooker pot.

Add the onion to the skillet and fry, stirring, for 5 minutes or until softened and just beginning to turn golden. Stir in the flour, then gradually mix in the stock. Add the Worcestershire sauce, tomato paste, mustard, and leaves from 2 sprigs of the rosemary. Season and bring to a boil, stirring.

Add the diced vegetables to the slow cooker pot. Pour the onions and sauce over them, then cover with the potato slices, arranging them so that they overlap and pressing them down into the stock. Sprinkle with the leaves torn from the remaining stem of rosemary and a little salt and black pepper.

Cover and cook on high for 7–8 hours, until the potatoes are tender. Lift the pot out of the housing using oven mitts, dot the potatoes with the butter, and brown under a hot broiler, if liked.

For chicken & blood sausage hotchpotch, replace the beef with 1¼ lb chicken thighs that have been skinned, boned, and diced. Continue as above, adding 3½ oz diced blood sausage along with the root vegetables. Cover with the potatoes and cook as above.

minted lamb with couscous

Preparation time **25 minutes**
Cooking temperature **high**
Cooking time **7–8 hours**
Serves **4**

1 tablespoon **olive oil**
½ **shoulder** of **lamb**
 (1 lb 14 oz–2 lb)
1 **onion**, sliced
2 **garlic cloves**, finely
 chopped
2 tablespoons **all-purpose**
 flour
3 tablespoons **mint jelly**
⅔ cup **red wine**
1¼ cups **lamb stock**
salt and **black pepper**

Herby couscous
1 cup **couscous**
1 cup peeled and diced
 cooked **beets**
1¾ cups boiling **water**
grated rind and juice of
 1 lemon
2 tablespoons **olive oil**
small bunch of **parsley**, finely
 chopped
small bunch of **mint**, finely
 chopped

Preheat the slow cooker, if necessary; see the
manufacturer's instructions. Heat the oil in a skillet, add
the lamb, and fry on both sides until browned. Lift out
with two slotted spoons and transfer to the slow cooker
pot. Fry the onion, stirring, for 5 minutes or until
softened and just turning golden.

Stir in the garlic, then the flour. Add the mint jelly and
wine and mix until smooth. Pour in the stock, season,
and bring to a boil, stirring. Pour the sauce over the lamb,
cover with the lid, and cook on high for 7–8 hours or
until the lamb is almost falling off the bone.

When almost ready to serve, put the couscous and
beets into a bowl, pour over the boiling water, then
add the lemon rind and juice, oil, and some seasoning.
Cover with a plate and let soak for 5 minutes.

Add the herbs to the couscous and fluff up with a fork,
then spoon onto plates. Lift the lamb onto a serving
plate and carve into rough pieces, discarding the
bone. Divide between the plates and serve the
sauce separately in a jug to pour over as needed.

For coriander & honey-braised lamb, fry the
onion and garlic as above. Add 1 tablespoon
roughly crushed coriander seeds with the flour. Stir in
1 tablespoon honey instead of the mint jelly and ⅔ cup
dry white wine instead of red. Add the lamb stock,
1 bay leaf, and seasoning. Bring to a boil, then add to
the browned lamb in the slow cooker pot. Cover and
cook as above. Serve with rice and green beans.

chicken korma

Preparation time **20 minutes**
Cooking temperature **low**
Cooking time **6–8 hours**
Serves **4**

2 tablespoons **sunflower oil**
8 **chicken thighs**, about 2 lb
　in total, skinned, boned,
　and cubed
2 **onions**, finely chopped, plus
　extra to garnish
1–2 **green chilies** (to taste),
　seeded and finely chopped
1 inch **fresh ginger**, peeled
　and finely chopped
⅛ cup **korma curry paste**
1 cup **coconut milk**
1¼ cups **chicken stock**
2 tablespoons **ground
　almonds**
small bunch of **cilantro**
1 cup **plain yogurt**
2 **tomatoes**, diced
salt and **black pepper**
warm **chapatis**, to serve

Preheat the slow cooker, if necessary; see the manufacturer's instructions. Heat the oil in a skillet, add the chicken a few pieces at time until it is all in the skillet, then fry, stirring, until golden. Remove from the skillet with a slotted spoon and put in the slow cooker pot.

Add the onions, green chilies, ginger, and curry paste to the skillet and fry, stirring, for 2–3 minutes. Pour in the coconut milk, stock, and ground almonds. Tear half the cilantro into pieces and add to the sauce with a little salt and black pepper. Bring to a boil, stirring, then spoon over the chicken.

Cover with the lid and cook on low for 6–8 hours. Stir the korma then ladle into bowls, top with spoonfuls of yogurt, the tomatoes and extra raw onion, and the remaining cilantro torn into small pieces. Serve with warm chapatis.

For fish korma, omit the chicken and fry the onions, chilies, ginger, and curry paste in the oil as above. Mix in the coconut milk, 1¼ cups fish stock instead of chicken stock, and the ground almonds, cilantro, and salt and black pepper. Bring to a boil, then pour into the slow cooker pot. Add 2 large cod loins, about 1 lb in total, press beneath the sauce, and cook on low for 2–2¼ hours or until the fish flakes when pressed with a knife.

steak & mushroom pie

Preparation time **40 minutes**
Cooking temperature **high**
Cooking time **5–6 hours**
Serves **4**

2 tablespoons **butter**, plus
   extra for greasing
1 tablespoon **sunflower oil**
2 large **onions**, roughly
   chopped
2 teaspoons **superfine sugar**
1½ cups sliced **cup
   mushrooms**
1 tablespoon **all-purpose** or
   self-rising flour
⅔ cup hot **beef stock**
1 teaspoon **Dijon mustard**
1 tablespoon **Worcestershire
   sauce**
1 lb 6 oz **round steak**, thinly
   sliced and any fat discarded
salt and **black pepper**

Pastry dough
2⅓ cups **self-rising flour**
½ teaspoon **salt**
¾ cup **lard**
scant 1 cup **water**

Preheat the slow cooker, if necessary; see the
manufacturer's instructions. Heat the butter and oil in
a skillet, add the onions, and fry for 5 minutes or until
softened. Sprinkle the sugar over the onions and fry for
5 more minutes or until browned. Add the mushrooms
and fry for 2–3 minutes. Stir in the flour.

Mix together the stock, mustard, Worcestershire sauce,
and salt and black pepper in a pitcher.

Make the pastry dough. Put the flour, salt, and lard
in a bowl and mix well. Gradually stir in enough water to
make a soft but not sticky dough. Knead the dough lightly,
then roll out on a floured surface to a circle 13 inches
across. Cut out a quarter segment and reserve.

Press the remaining dough into a 1½ quart buttered
ovenproof bowl, butting the edges together.

Layer the fried onions, mushrooms, and sliced steak in the
bowl. Pour the stock over the top. Pat the reserved dough
into a round the same size as the top of the bowl. Fold the
top edges of the dough in the bowl over the filling, brush
with a little water and cover with the dough lid.

Cover the pie with a large domed circle of buttered
foil so that there is room for the pastry to rise. Tie with
kitchen twine. Stand the bowl in the slow cooker pot on
top of an upturned saucer. Pour boiling water into the
pot to come halfway up the sides of the bowl. Cover
with the lid and cook on high for 5–6 hours.

Remove the bowl from the slow cooker using a tea
towel and remove the twine and foil. The pastry should
have risen and feel dry to the touch.

rancheros pie

Preparation time **25 minutes**
Cooking temperature **low**
Cooking time **7–8 hours**
Serves **4**

1 tablespoon **sunflower oil**
1 lb **ground beef**
1 **onion**, chopped
2 **garlic cloves**, finely
   chopped
1 teaspoon **cumin seeds**,
   roughly crushed
¼–½ teaspoon **crushed dried
   red chilies**
¼ teaspoon **ground allspice**
2 stems of **oregano**, roughly
   chopped
3 tablespoons **golden raisins**
13 oz canned **chopped
   tomatoes**
1 cup **beef stock**
salt and **black pepper**

Topping
2 large (1 lb) **sweet potatoes**,
   thinly sliced
2 tablespoons **butter**
few **crushed dried red chilies**

Preheat the slow cooker, if necessary; see the
manufacturer's instructions. Heat the oil in a skillet,
add the beef and onion, and fry, stirring and breaking
up the meat with a wooden spoon, until browned.

Stir in the garlic, spices, oregano, raisins, tomatoes,
and stock. Add a little salt and black pepper and bring
to a boil, stirring. Spoon into the slow cooker pot, cover
with overlapping slices of sweet potato, dot with butter,
and sprinkle with dried chilies and a little salt and
black pepper.

Cover with the lid and cook on low for 7–8 hours,
until the potato topping is tender. Lift the pot out of
the housing using oven mitts and brown under a hot
broiler, if liked.

For cowboy pie, fry the beef and onion as above,
then omit the garlic, spices, oregano, golden raisins,
and tomatoes but add 2 tablespoons Worcestershire
sauce, 13½ oz canned baked beans, 1 bay leaf, and
1 cup beef stock. Cook the beef base as above. Top
with 6 medium (1½ lb) potatoes, cooked and mashed
with butter and salt and black pepper. Sprinkle with
½ cup shredded cheddar cheese and brown under
the grill.

caribbean chicken with rice & peas

Preparation time **20 minutes**
Cooking temperature **low** and
  high
Cooking time **7–9 hours**
Serves **4**

8 **chicken thighs**, about 2 lb
  in total
3 tablespoons **jerk marinade**
  (see below)
2 tablespoons **sunflower oil**
2 large **onions**, chopped
2 **garlic cloves**, finely
  chopped
2 cups **coconut milk**
1½ cups **chicken stock**
13½ oz canned **red kidney
  beans**, drained
1 cup instant **long-grain rice**
scant 1 cup frozen **peas**
salt and **black pepper**

To garnish
lime wedges
sprigs of **cilantro**

Preheat the slow cooker, if necessary; see the manufacturer's instructions. Remove the skin from the chicken thighs, slash each thigh 2–3 times, and rub with the jerk marinade.

Heat 1 tablespoon oil in a large skillet, add the chicken, and fry over a high heat until browned on both sides. Lift out with a slotted spoon and transfer to a plate. Add the remaining oil, the onions, and garlic, reduce the heat, and fry for 5 minutes or until softened and lightly browned. Pour in the coconut milk and stock, season with salt and black pepper, and bring to a boil.

Transfer half the mixture to the slow cooker pot, add half the chicken pieces, all the beans, and then the remaining chicken, onions, and coconut mixture. Cover, cook on low for 6–8 hours, until the chicken is tender.

Stir in the rice, replace the lid, and cook on high for 45 minutes. Add the frozen peas (no need to thaw) and cook for another 15 minutes. Spoon on to plates and serve garnished with lime wedges and cilantro sprigs.

For jerk marinade, halve 1–2 scotch bonnet chilies, depending on their size, discard the seeds, and chop finely. Put in a clean screw-top jar with 1 tablespoon finely chopped thyme leaves, 1 teaspoon ground allspice, 1 teaspoon ground cinnamon, ½ teaspoon grated nutmeg, ½ teaspoon salt, ½ teaspoon ground black black pepper, 3 teaspoons brown sugar, 2 tablespoons sunflower oil, and ¼ cup cider vinegar. Screw on the lid tightly and shake to mix. Use 3 tablespoons of the marinade and store the remainder in the refrigerator for up to 2 weeks.

beef adobo

Preparation time **25 minutes**
Cooking temperature **low**
Cooking time **8–10 hours**
Serves **4**

1 tablespoon **sunflower oil**
1½ lb **braising beef**, cubed
   and any fat discarded
1 large **onion**, sliced
2 **garlic cloves**, finely
   chopped
2 tablespoons **all-purpose
   flour**
2 cups **beef stock**
¼ cup **soy sauce**
¼ cup **wine vinegar**
1 tablespoon **superfine sugar**
2 **bay leaves**
juice of 1 **lime**
salt and **black pepper**
long-grain rice, to serve

To garnish
1 **carrot**, cut into thin sticks
½ cup bunch of **scallions**, cut
   into shreds
cilantro leaves

Preheat the slow cooker, if necessary; see the manufacturer's instructions. Heat the oil in a large skillet and add the beef a few pieces at a time until all the meat has been added. Fry over high heat, turning until evenly browned, lift out of the pan with a slotted spoon and transfer to a plate.

Add the onion to the skillet and fry for 5 minutes or until it is just beginning to brown. Mix in the garlic and cook for 2 minutes. Stir in the flour, then gradually mix in the stock. Add the soy sauce, vinegar, sugar, bay leaves, and salt and black pepper and bring to a boil, stirring.

Transfer the beef to the slow cooker pot, pour over the onion and stock mixture, cover with the lid, and cook on low for 8–10 hours.

Stir in lime juice to taste and garnish with carrot sticks, shredded scallions and cilantro leaves. Serve in shallow bowls lined with rice.

For hoisin beef, combine 3 tablespoons each soy sauce and rice or wine vinegar with 2 tablespoons hoisin sauce and 1 inch peeled and finely chopped fresh ginger. Add this mixture to the beef stock with the sugar. Omit the bay leaves. Bring the mixture to a boil, then continue as above, adding the lime juice just before serving.

lamb tagine with figs & almonds

Preparation time **15 minutes**
Cooking temperature **low**
Cooking time **8–10 hours**
Serves **4**

1 tablespoon **olive oil**
1½ lb **lamb fillet**, diced, or
   diced lamb
1 **onion**, sliced
2 **garlic cloves**, finely
   chopped
1 inch **fresh ginger**, peeled
   and finely chopped
2 tablespoons **all-purpose
   flour**
2½ cups **lamb stock**
1 teaspoon **ground cinnamon**
2 large pinches of **saffron
   threads**
⅓ cup diced dried **figs**, stalks
   trimmed off
¼ cup **toasted slivered
   almonds**
salt and **black pepper**

Preheat the slow cooker, if necessary; see the
manufacturer's handbook. Heat the oil in a skillet, add
the lamb a few pieces at a time until all the pieces are
added to the skillet, then fry over high heat, stirring until
browned. Remove from the skillet with a slotted spoon
and transfer to the slow cooker pot.

Add the onion and fry, stirring, for 5 minutes or until
softened and just beginning to turn golden. Stir in the
garlic and ginger, then mix in the flour. Gradually stir
in the stock. Add the spices, figs, and a little salt and
black pepper and bring to a boil, stirring.

Spoon into the slow cooker pot, cover with the lid, and
cook on low for 8–10 hours or until the lamb is tender.
Stir, then sprinkle with toasted slivered almonds. Serve
with lemon and chickpea couscous (see below).

For lemon & chickpea couscous to accompany
the tagine put 1 cup couscous into a bowl, add the
grated rind and juice of 1 lemon, 2 tablespoons olive
oil, drained 13½ oz canned chickpeas (garbanzo
beans), and some salt and black pepper. Pour over
2 cups boiling water, then cover the bowl with a plate
and let stand for 5 minutes. Remove the plate, add
1¾ cups chopped parsley or cilantro and fluff up
with a fork.

lemon chicken

Preparation time **20 minutes**
Cooking temperature **high**
Cooking time **3¼–4¼ hours**
Serves **4**

1 tablespoon **olive oil**
4 boneless, skinless **chicken breasts**, about 1 lb 2 oz in total
1 **onion**, chopped
2 **garlic cloves**, finely chopped
2 tablespoons **all-purpose flour**
2 cups **chicken stock**
½ **lemon** (cut in half lengthwise), cut into 4 wedges
2 **bok choy**, thickly sliced
1¼ cups **sugar snap peas**, halved lengthwise
¼ cup **crème fraîche (**or 2 tablespoons whipping cream mixed with 2 tablespoons sour cream)
2 tablespoons chopped **mint** and **parsley**, mixed
salt and **black pepper**

To serve
couscous mixed with finely chopped **tomato, red onion, and red bell pepper**

Preheat the slow cooker, if necessary; see the manufacturer's instructions. Heat the oil in a large skillet, add the chicken breasts, and fry over a high heat until browned on both sides. Remove from the skillet and transfer to a plate. Add the onion to the skillet and fry, stirring, for 5 minutes or until lightly browned.

Stir in the garlic and flour, then mix in the stock and lemon wedges. Season with salt and black pepper and bring to a boil.

Put the chicken breasts in the slow cooker pot, pour the hot stock mixture over them, and press the chicken below the surface of the liquid. Cover with the lid and cook on high for 3–4 hours.

Add the bok choy and sugar snap peas and cook, still on high, for 15 minutes or until just tender. Lift out the chicken, slice the pieces, and arrange them on plates. Stir the crème fraîche and herbs into the sauce, then spoon it and the vegetables over the chicken. Serve with couscous mixed with finely chopped tomato, red onion, and red bell pepper.

For lemon chicken with harissa, add 4 teaspoons harissa paste to the skillet with the chicken stock and wedges cut from ½ lemon. Continue as above. Omit the bok choy at the end, adding instead 1¾ cups broccoli, the florets cut into small pieces and stems sliced, and ½ zucchini. Reduce the sugar snap peas to just ½ cup .

olive & lemon meatballs

Preparation time **30 minutes**
Cooking temperature **low**
Cooking time **6–8 hours**
Serves **4**

Meatballs
⅓ cup chopped, pitted
   black olives
grated rind of ½ **lemon**
1 lb **extra-lean ground beef**
1 **egg yolk**
1 tablespoon **olive oil**

Sauce
1 **onion**, chopped
2 **garlic cloves**, finely
   chopped
13 oz canned **chopped
   tomatoes**
1 teaspoon **superfine sugar**
⅔ cup **chicken stock**
salt and **black pepper**
small **basil leaves**, to garnish
tagliatelle tossed with
   chopped **basil** and **melted
   butter**, to serve

Preheat the slow cooker, if necessary; see the manufacturer's instructions. Make the meatballs. Put all the ingredients except for the oil in a bowl and mix with a wooden spoon. Wet your hands and shape the mixture into 20 balls.

Heat the oil in a large skillet, add the meatballs and cook over high heat, turning until browned on all sides. Lift them out of pan with a slotted spoon and transfer to a plate.

Make the sauce. Add the onion to the skillet and fry, stirring, for 5 minutes or until lightly browned. Add the garlic, tomatoes, sugar, stock, and salt and black pepper and bring to a boil, stirring.

Transfer the meatballs to the slow cooker pot, pour over the hot sauce, cover, and cook on low for 6–8 hours. Garnish with basil leaves and serve with tagliatelle tossed with chopped basil and melted butter.

For herb & garlic meatballs, replace the olives and lemon rind with 2 finely chopped garlic cloves and 3 tablespoons chopped basil leaves. Mix, shape, and cook the meatballs with the sauce as above, adding a small handful of basil leaves to the sauce just before serving.

mustard chicken & bacon

Preparation time **15 minutes**
Cooking temperature **low**
Cooking time **8¼–10¼ hours**
Serves **4**

1 tablespoon **butter**
1 tablespoon **sunflower oil**
4 **chicken thigh** and
   4 **chicken drumstick** pieces
4 slices **smoked lean bacon**,
   diced
13 oz **leeks**, thinly sliced;
   white and green parts kept
   separate
2 tablespoons **all-purpose**
   flour
2½ cups **chicken stock**
3 teaspoons **whole-grain**
   mustard
salt and **black pepper**
mashed **potato**, to serve

Preheat the slow cooker, if necessary; see the manufacturer's instructions. Heat the butter and oil in a skillet, add the chicken pieces, and fry over high heat until browned on all sides. Transfer to the slow cooker pot with a slotted spoon.

Add the bacon and white sliced leeks to the skillet and fry, stirring, for 5 minutes or until just beginning to turn golden. Stir in the flour, then gradually mix in the stock, mustard, and a little salt and black pepper. Bring to a boil. Pour into the slow cooker pot, cover with the lid, and cook on low for 8–10 hours.

Add the green sliced leeks and stir into the sauce, then replace the lid and cook, still on low, for 15 minutes or until the green leeks are just softened. Spoon into shallow serving bowls and serve with mashed potato.

For mustard chicken & frankfurter casserole, fry the chicken as above, then drain and add to the slow cooker pot. Add 1 chopped onion to the skillet, then mix in 4 chilled, sliced frankfurters and fry for 5 minutes. Stir in the flour, then mix in the stock, mustard and seasoning as above. Add 7 oz canned drained corn kernels, transfer to the slow cooker pot, and cook on low for 8–10 hours.

beery barley beef

Preparation time **15 minutes**
Cooking temperature **low**
Cooking time **9–10 hours**
Serves **4**

1 tablespoon **sunflower oil**
1¼ lb lean **braising beef**,
  cubed
1 **onion**, chopped
1 tablespoon **all-purpose
  flour**
4 medium **carrots**, diced
2 medium **parsnips** or
  potatoes, diced
1¼ cups **light ale**
3 cups **beef stock**
small bunch of **mixed herbs**
  or dried **bouquet garni**
½ cup **pearl barley**
salt and **black pepper**

Preheat the slow cooker, if necessary; see the manufacturer's instructions. Heat the oil in a skillet, add the beef a few pieces at a time until it is all in the pan, then fry over a high heat, stirring, until browned. Remove the beef with a slotted spoon and transfer to the slow cooker pot.

Add the onion to the skillet and fry, stirring, for 5 minutes or until lightly browned. Mix in the flour, then add the root vegetables and beer and bring to a boil, stirring. Pour into the slow cooker pot.

Add the stock to the skillet with the herbs and a little salt and black pepper, bring to a boil, then pour into the slow cooker pot. Add the pearl barley, cover with the lid, and cook on low for 9–10 hours until the beef is tender. Serve with herb croutons (see below), if liked.

For herb croutons to accompany the beef, beat 2 tablespoons chopped parsley, 2 tablespoons chopped chives, and 1 tablespoon chopped tarragon and a little black black pepper into 6 tablespoons soft butter. Thickly slice ½ French bread, toast lightly on both sides, then spread with the herb butter.

pheasant pot-roast with chestnuts

Preparation time **15 minutes**
Cooking temperature **high**
Cooking time **3–4 hours**
Serves **2–3**

1 **pheasant**, about 1½ lb
2 tablespoons **butter**
1 tablespoon **olive oil**
7 oz **shallots**, halved
2 oz **smoked fatty bacon**,
   diced, or diced **pancetta**
2 **celery ribs**, thickly sliced
1 tablespoon **all-purpose**
   flour
1¼ cups **chicken stock**
¼ cup **dry sherry**
3½ oz vacuum-packed
   prepared **chestnuts**
2–3 sprigs of **thyme**
salt and **black pepper**
potatoes dauphinois,
   to serve

Preheat the slow cooker, if necessary; see the manufacturer's instructions. Rinse the pheasant inside and out with plenty of cold running water, then pat dry with paper towels.

Heat the butter and oil in a skillet, add the pheasant, breast side down, the shallots, bacon or pancetta, and celery and fry until golden brown, turning the pheasant and stirring the other ingredients. Transfer the pheasant to the slow cooker pot, placing it breast side down.

Stir the flour into the onion mix. Gradually add the stock and sherry, then add the chestnuts, thyme, and a little salt and black pepper. Bring to a boil, stirring, then spoon over the pheasant. Cover with the lid and cook on high for 3–4 hours, until tender. Test with a knife through the thickest part of the pheasant leg and breast to make sure that the juices run clear. Carve the pheasant breast into thick slices and cut the legs away from the body. Serve with potatoes dauphinois.

For guinea fowl pot-roast with dried plums (prunes), fry a 2 lb guinea fowl instead of the pheasant as above. Transfer the fowl to the slow cooker, mix in 2 tablespoons all-purpose flour, then add 2 cups chicken stock and the sherry. Omit the chestnuts, and add 3 oz halved, pitted dried plums (prunes) instead. Continue as above, but cook for 5–6 hours.

fish & seafood

caribbean brown stew trout

Preparation time **20 minutes**
Cooking temperature **high**
Cooking time **1½–2 hours**
Serves **4**

4 small **trout**, gutted, heads
   and fins removed, and well
   rinsed with cold water
1 teaspoon **ground allspice**
1 teaspoon **paprika**
1 teaspoon **ground coriander**
2 tablespoons **olive oil**
6 **scallions**, thickly sliced
1 **red bell pepper**, cored,
   seeded, and thinly sliced
2 **tomatoes**, roughly chopped
½ **red hot bonnet** or other **red
   chili**, seeded and chopped
2 sprigs of **thyme**
1¼ cups **fish stock**
salt and **black pepper**

Preheat the slow cooker, if necessary; see the manufacturer's instructions. Slash the trout on each side 2–3 times with a sharp knife. Mix the spices and a little salt and black pepper on a plate, then dip each side of the trout in the spice mix.

Heat the oil in a skillet, add the trout, and fry until browned on both sides but not cooked all the way through. Drain and arrange in the slow cooker pot with the fish resting on their lower edges and alternating heads and tails so that they fit snugly in a single layer.

Add the remaining ingredients to the skillet with any spices left on the plate and bring to a boil, stirring. Pour over the trout, then cover with the lid and cook on high for 1½–2 hours or until the fish breaks into flakes when pressed in the center with a knife.

Lift the fish carefully out of the slow cooker pot, using a fish spatula and transfer to shallow dishes. Spoon the sauce over and serve with warm bread to mop up the sauce, if liked.

For brown stew chicken, slash 8 chicken thigh pieces instead of the trout and dip in the spice mix as above. Fry in the olive oil until browned, then drain and transfer to the slow cooker pot. Heat the vegetables as above with 2 cups chicken stock, season, then cook with the chicken pieces in the slow cooker on low for 8–10 hours. Thicken the sauce, if liked, with 4 teaspoons cornstarch mixed with a little water by stirring it into the sauce and cooking for 15 minutes more.

hot soused herrings

Preparation time **15 minutes**
Cooking temperature **high**
Cooking time **1½–2 hours**
Serves **4**

1 large **red onion**, thinly sliced
1 large **carrot**, cut into
    matchsticks
1 large **celery rib**, thinly sliced
6 small **herrings**, gutted,
    filleted, and rinsed with
    cold water
2 stems of **tarragon**
1 **bay leaf**
⅔ cup **cider vinegar**
2 tablespoons **superfine
    sugar**
2½ cups boiling **water**
½ teaspoon colored
    peppercorns
salt
tarragon sprigs, to garnish

Preheat the slow cooker, if necessary; see the manufacturer's instructions. Put half the onion, carrot, and celery in the bottom of the slow cooker pot. Arrange the herring fillets on top, then cover with the remaining vegetables.

Add the tarragon, bay leaf, vinegar, and sugar, then pour over the boiling water. Add the peppercorns and a little salt. Cover with the lid and cook on high for 1½–2 hours.

Spoon the fish, vegetables, and a little of the cooking liquid into shallow bowls, halving the fish fillets, if liked. Garnish with tarragon sprigs. Serve with pickled beets, dill pickles, and bread and butter, if liked.

For Swedish baked herrings, make as above, adding 2 sprigs of dill instead of the tarragon and increasing the amount of sugar to ¼ cup. Let cool once cooked and serve with ½ cup sour cream mixed with 1 teaspoon hot horseradish and accompanied by a pickle salad.

salmon in hot miso broth

Preparation time **15 minutes**

Cooking temperature **low** and
   high

Cooking time **1 hour
   40 minutes–2 hours
   10 minutes**

Serves 6

4 **salmon steaks**, about
   4 oz each

1 **carrot**, thinly sliced

4 **scallions**, thinly sliced

4 **cup mushrooms**, about
   4 oz in total, thinly sliced

1 large **red chili**, halved,
   seeded, and finely chopped

¾ inch **fresh ginger**, peeled
   and finely chopped

3 tablespoons **miso**

1 tablespoon dark **soy sauce**

2 tablespoons **mirin** (optional)

5 cups hot **fish stock**

¾ cup **snow peas**, thinly
   sliced

cilantro leaves, to garnish

Preheat the slow cooker, if necessary; see the manufacturer's instructions. Rinse the salmon in cold water, drain, and place in the slow cooker pot. Arrange the carrot, scallions, mushrooms, chili, and ginger on top of the fish.

Add the miso, soy sauce, and mirin (if used) to the hot stock and stir until the miso has dissolved. Pour the stock mixture over the salmon and vegetables. Cover with the lid and cook on low for 1½–2 hours or until the fish is tender and the soup is piping hot.

Lift the fish out with a spatula and transfer it to a plate. Flake it into chunky pieces, discarding the skin and any bones. Return the fish to the slow cooker pot and add the snow peas. Cook on high for 10 minutes or until the snow peas are just tender, then ladle the soup into bowls and garnish with cilantro leaves.

For salmon in aromatic Thai broth, follow the recipe as above, adding 3 teaspoons Thai red curry paste, 3 small kaffir lime leaves, and 2 teaspoons Thai fish sauce instead of the miso and mirin.

mackerel with harissa potatoes

Preparation time **20 minutes**
Cooking temperature **low**
Cooking time **5–7 hours**
Serves **4**

1 lb **new potatoes**, scrubbed
   and thickly sliced
1 tablespoon **olive oil**
1 **onion**, chopped
½ **red bell pepper**, cored,
   seeded, and diced
½ **yellow bell pepper**, cored,
   seeded and diced
1 **garlic clove**, finely chopped
2 teaspoons **harissa**
   (Moroccan chili paste)
2 small **tomatoes**, roughly
   chopped
1 tablespoon **tomato paste**
1¼ cups **fish stock**
4 small **mackerel**, each about
   10 oz, gutted and heads
   removed
salt and **black pepper**

Preheat the slow cooker, if necessary; see the
manufacturer's instructions. Bring a saucepan of water
to a boil, add the potatoes, and cook for 4–5 minutes
or until almost tender. Drain and reserve.

Heat the oil in a skillet, add the onion, and fry, stirring,
for 5 minutes or until softened and just beginning to
turn golden. Stir in the bell peppers and garlic and fry
for 2–3 minutes. Mix in the harissa, tomatoes, tomato
paste, stock, and a little salt and black pepper, and
bring to a boil.

Turn the potatoes into the bottom of the slow cooker
pot. Rinse the fish well, drain, and arrange in a single
layer on top of the potatoes, then cover with the hot
tomato mixture. Cover with the lid and cook on low for
5–7 hours or until the potatoes are tender and the fish
flakes when pressed in the center with a small knife.

Spoon into shallow bowls and serve with warmed
pitta breads, if liked.

For harissa-spiced potatoes with feta, follow
the recipe as above but omit the fish and instead
sprinkle the top of the tomato mixture with 4 oz
drained and crumbled feta cheese and ⅓ cup pitted
black olives. Cook as above and sprinkle with torn
parsley just before serving.

macaroni with smoked haddock

Preparation time **15 minutes**
Cooking temperature **low**
Cooking time **2¼–3¼ hours**
Serves **4**

7 oz **macaroni**
1 tablespoon **olive oil**
1 **onion**, chopped
4 tablespoons **butter**
⅛ cup **all-purpose flour**
scant 2 cups **long life
(UHT) milk**
scant 2 cups **fish stock**
1½ cups shredded **cheddar
cheese**
¼ teaspoon grated **nutmeg**
1 lb **smoked haddock**,
skinned and cut into
1 inch cubes
7 oz canned **corn kernels**,
drained
4 cups rinsed, drained, and
roughly torn **fresh spinach**
salt and **black pepper**
grilled **cherry tomatoes** on
the vine, to serve

Preheat the slow cooker, if necessary; see the manufacturer's instructions. Put the macaroni into a bowl, cover with plenty of boiling water, and let stand for 10 minutes while preparing the rest of the dish.

Heat the oil in a saucepan, add the onion, and fry gently, stirring, for 5 minutes or until softened. Add the butter and, when melted, stir in the flour. Gradually mix in the milk and bring to a boil, stirring until smooth. Stir in the stock, 1 cup of the cheese, nutmeg and salt and black pepper, and bring back to the boil, stirring.

Drain the macaroni and add to the slow cooker pot with the haddock and corn kernels. Pour over the sauce and gently stir together. Cover with the lid and cook on low for 2–3 hours.

Stir the spinach into the macaroni, replace the lid, and cook on low for 15 minutes. Lift the pot out of the housing, using oven mitts and stir once more. Sprinkle the remaining cheese over the macaroni, then brown under a hot broiler until the top is golden. Serve with broiled cherry tomatoes on the vine.

For Stilton macaroni with bacon, soak the macaroni as above. Make up the cheese sauce with the milk, adding vegetable stock in place of fish stock and replacing the cheddar cheese with Stilton cheese. Omit the fish and cook as above with the corn kernels. Stir in the spinach and 6 slices broiled smoked lean bacon, diced. Cook for 15 minutes, then finish with a little extra Stilton and brown under the broiler.

tuna arrabiata

Preparation time **20 minutes**
Cooking temperature **low**
Cooking time **4–5 hours**
Serves 4

1 tablespoon **olive oil**
1 **onion**, chopped
2 **garlic cloves**, finely
   chopped
1 **red bell pepper**, cored,
   seeded, and diced
1 teaspoon **smoked paprika**
   (pimenton)
¼–½ teaspoon **crushed dried
   red chilies**
13 oz canned **chopped
   tomatoes**
⅔ cup **vegetable** or **fish stock**
7 oz canned **tuna** in water,
   drained
12 oz **spaghetti**
salt and **black pepper**

To serve
freshly grated **Parmesan
   cheese**
basil leaves

Preheat the slow cooker, if necessary; see the
manufacturer's instructions. Heat the oil in a skillet,
add the onion, and fry, stirring, for 5 minutes or until
just beginning to turn golden around the edges.

Stir in the garlic, red bell pepper, paprika, and dried
chilies and cook for 2 minutes. Mix in the tomatoes,
stock, and a little salt and black pepper. Bring to a boil,
then put into the slow cooker pot. Break the tuna into
large pieces and stir into the tomato mixture. Cover
with the lid and cook on low for 4–5 hours.

When almost ready to serve, bring a large saucepan
of water to a boil, add the spaghetti, and cook for about
8 minutes or until tender. Drain and stir into the tomato
sauce. Spoon into shallow bowls and sprinkle with
grated Parmesan and basil leaves to taste.

For double tomato arrabiata, omit the tuna from the
tomato sauce. Instead, mix in ¾ cup sliced sun-dried
tomatoes and 1⅓ cups sliced white mushrooms. Cook
and serve as above.

chermoula poached salmon

Preparation time **15 minutes**
Cooking temperature **low**
Cooking time **1¾–2¼ hours**
Serves **4**

6 **scallions**
¼ bunch of Italian **parsley**
⅛ bunch **cilantro**
grated rind and juice of
  1 **lemon**
¼ cup **olive oil**
½ teaspoon **cumin seeds**,
  roughly crushed
1 lb thick end **salmon fillet**
  no longer than 7 inches,
  skinned
1 cup **fish stock**
⅛ cup **mayonnaise**
4 oz mixed **salad greens**
salt and **black pepper**

Preheat the slow cooker, if necessary; see the manufacturer's instructions. Finely chop the scallions and herbs with a large knife or in a food processor, if you have one. Mix with the lemon rind and juice, the oil, cumin seeds, and a little salt and black pepper.

Rinse the salmon with cold water, drain well, and put on a long piece of kitchen foil, the width of the salmon. Press half the herb mixture over both sides of the salmon, then use the foil to lower the fish into the slow cooker pot.

Bring the stock to a boil in a small saucepan, pour over the salmon, and tuck the ends of the foil down, if needed. Cover with the lid and cook on low for 1¾–2¼ hours or until the fish flakes into opaque pieces when pressed in the center with a knife.

Lift the salmon out of the slow cooker pot using the foil and transfer to a serving plate. Mix the remaining uncooked herb mixture with the mayonnaise. Arrange the salad greens on 4 plates. Cut the salmon into 4 pieces and place on the salad. Serve with spoonfuls of the herb mayonnaise.

For classic poached salmon, omit the chermoula herb mixture. Rinse the salmon as above, then lower into the slow cooker pot on a piece of foil. Add ½ sliced lemon, ½ sliced onion, 2 sprigs of tarragon, and a little salt and black pepper. Bring 1 cup fish stock and ¼ cup white wine to a boil in a small saucepan, pour over the fish, and cook as above. Drain and serve hot or cold with salad and spoonfuls of plain mayonnaise.

squid in puttanesca sauce

Preparation time **25 minutes**
Cooking temperature **low**
Cooking time **3½–4½ hours**
Serves **4**

1 lb prepared **squid tubes**
1 tablespoon **olive oil**
1 **onion**, chopped
2 **garlic cloves**, finely
  chopped
13 oz canned **chopped
  tomatoes**
⅔ cup **fish stock**
4 teaspoons **capers**, drained
⅓ cup pitted **black olives**
2–3 sprigs of **thyme**, plus
  extra to garnish (optional)
1 teaspoon **fennel seeds**,
  roughly crushed
1 teaspoon **superfine sugar**
salt and **black pepper**
linguine, to serve

Preheat the slow cooker, if necessary; see the manufacturer's instructions. Take the tentacles out of the squid tubes and rinse inside the tubes with cold water. Put them in a strainer and rinse the outside of the tubes and the tentacles. Drain well, put the tentacles in a small bowl, cover, and return to the refrigerator. Thickly slice the squid tubes.

Heat the oil in a large skillet, add the onion, and fry, stirring, for 5 minutes or until golden. Add the garlic and cook for 2 minutes. Stir in the tomatoes, stock, capers, olives, thyme, fennel seeds, sugar, and salt and black pepper and bring to a boil.

Pour the sauce into the slow cooker pot, add the sliced squid, and press the pieces below the surface of the sauce. Cover and cook on low for 3–4 hours.

Stir the squid mixture and add the tentacles, pressing them below the surface of the sauce. Cook on low for 30 minutes. Serve tossed with linguine and garnished with extra thyme leaves, if liked.

For squid in red wine & tomato sauce, replace the stock, capers, olives, and fennel seeds with ⅔ cup red wine. Cook as above, then garnish with chopped parsley and serve with warm crusty bread.

smoked mackerel kedgeree

Preparation time **15 minutes**
Cooking temperature **low**
Cooking time **3¼–4¼ hours**
Serves **4**

1 tablespoon **sunflower oil**
1 **onion**, chopped
1 teaspoon **turmeric**
2 tablespoons **mango chutney**
3–3¾ cups **vegetable stock**
1 **bay leaf**
¾ cup plus 2 tablespoons instant **brown rice**
8 oz or **3 smoked mackerel fillets**, skinned
⅔ cup frozen **peas**
1½ cups **watercress** or **arugula** leaves
4 **hard-cooked eggs**, cut into wedges
salt and **black pepper**

Preheat the slow cooker if necessary; see the manufacturer's instructions. Heat the oil in a skillet, add the onion, and fry, stirring, for 5 minutes or until softened and just beginning to turn golden.

Stir in the turmeric, chutney, stock, bay leaf, and a little salt and black pepper and bring to a boil. Pour into the slow cooker pot and add the rice. Add the smoked mackerel to the pot in a single layer. Cover with the lid and cook on low for 3–4 hours or until the rice is tender and has absorbed almost all the stock.

Stir in the peas, breaking up the fish into chunky pieces. Add extra hot stock if needed. Cook for 15 minutes more. Stir in the watercress or arugula, spoon onto plates, and garnish with wedges of egg.

For smoked haddock kedgeree with cardamom, make up the recipe as above but omit the mango chutney and instead add 4 crushed cardamom pods with their black seeds. Replace the smoked mackerel with 13 oz skinned smoked haddock fillet, cut into 2 pieces. Continue as above, adding the peas and egg wedges at the end but omitting the arugula or watercress. Drizzle with ¼ cup heavy cream.

poached salmon with beurre blanc

Preparation time **25 minutes**
Cooking temperature **low**
Cooking time **1¾–2¼ hours**
Serves **4**

7 tablespoons **butter**
1 large **onion**, thinly sliced
1 **lemon**, sliced
1 lb piece of thick end **salmon fillet**, no longer than 7 inches
1 **bay leaf**
scant 1 cup dry **white wine**
1¼ cups **fish stock**
3 tablespoons finely chopped **chives**, plus extra to garnish
salt and **black pepper**
lemon slices, to garnish

Preheat the slow cooker, if necessary; see the manufacturer's instructions. Brush inside the slow cooker pot with a little of the butter. Fold a large piece of kitchen foil into 3, then place it at the bottom of the pot with the ends sticking up to use as a strap. Arrange the onion slices and half of the lemon slices over the foil. Place the salmon, flesh side up, on top. Season with salt and black pepper, then add the bay leaf and remaining lemon slices.

Pour the wine and stock into a saucepan, bring to a boil, then pour over the salmon. Fold the foil down, if necessary, to fit the cooker lid, then cook on low for 1¾–2¼ hours, until the fish is opaque and flakes easily when pressed in the center with a knife.

Lift the salmon carefully out of the pot, using the foil strap, draining off as much liquid as possible. Transfer to a serving plate, discard the bay leaf, lemon, and onion slices, and keep warm. Strain the cooking liquid into a saucepan and boil rapidly for 4–5 minutes or until reduced to about ¼ cup.

Reduce the heat and gradually whisk in small pieces of the remaining butter, little by little, until the sauce thickens and becomes creamy. (Don't be tempted to rush making the sauce either by adding the butter all at once or by increasing the heat to the sauce, or you may find that it separates.) Stir in the chopped chives and adjust the seasoning, if needed.

Cut the salmon into 4 portions, discard the skin, and transfer to individual plates. Spoon a little of the sauce around the fish. Garnish with lemon slices and chives.

vegetables

herby stuffed bell peppers

Preparation time **20 minutes**
Cooking temperature **low**
Cooking time **4–5 hours**
Serves **4**

4 different colored **bell peppers**
½ cup instant **brown rice**
13½ oz canned **chickpeas (garbanzo beans)**, drained
small bunch of **parsley**, roughly chopped
small bunch of **mint**, roughly chopped
1 **onion**, finely chopped
2 **garlic cloves**, finely chopped
½ teaspoon **smoked paprika**
1 teaspoon **ground allspice**
2½ cups hot **vegetable stock**
salt and **black pepper**

Preheat the slow cooker, if necessary; see the manufacturer's instructions. Cut the top off each pepper, then remove the core and seeds.

Mix together the rice, chickpeas (garbanzo beans), herbs, onion, garlic, paprika, and allspice with plenty of seasoning. Spoon the mixture into the insides of the bell peppers, then put the peppers into the slow cooker pot.

Pour the hot stock around the bell peppers, cover with the lid, and cook on low for 4–5 hours or until the rice and peppers are tender. Spoon into dishes and serve with salad and spoonfuls of Greek yogurt flavored with extra chopped herbs, if liked.

For feta-stuffed peppers, make the recipe as above, but use 3½ oz crumbled feta cheese, ¼ cup golden raisins, a small bunch of chopped basil, and ¼ teaspoon ground allspice instead of the chopped parsley, mint, paprika, and allspice.

mushroom & walnut cobbler

Preparation time **30 minutes**
Cooking temperature **low** and
  high
Cooking time **6¾–8¾ hours**
Serves **4**

2 tablespoons **olive oil**
1 **onion**, chopped
2 **garlic cloves**, chopped
8 oz **flat mushrooms**, peeled
  and quartered
8 oz **cremini mushrooms**,
  quartered
1 tablespoon **all-purpose
  flour**
scant 1 cup **red wine**
13 oz canned **chopped
  tomatoes**
1¼ cups **vegetable stock**
1 tablespoon **red-currant jelly**
2–3 stems of **thyme**
salt and **black pepper**

Walnut topping
1⅔ cups **self-rising flour**
4 tablespoons **butter**, diced
⅓ cup chopped **walnut** pieces
⅔ cup shredded **cheddar
  cheese**
1 **egg**, beaten
4–5 tablespoons **milk**

Preheat the slow cooker, if necessary; see the manufacturer's instructions. Heat the oil in a skillet, add the onion, garlic, and mushrooms and fry, stirring, for 5 minutes or until just turning golden.

Stir in the flour, then mix in the wine, tomatoes, and stock. Add the red-currant jelly, thyme, and salt and black pepper and bring to a boil. Pour into the slow cooker pot, cover with the lid, and cook on low for 6–8 hours.

When almost ready to serve, make the topping. Put the flour and butter in a bowl, rub in the butter with your fingertips until fine bread crumbs form. Stir in the walnuts, cheese, and salt and black pepper. Add half the egg, then mix in enough milk to make a soft dough.

Knead lightly, then roll out the dough on a lightly floured surface until ¾ inch thick. Stamp out 8 rounds with a 2½ inch plain cookie cutter, rerolling trimmings as needed. Stir the mushroom casserole, then arrange the biscuits, slightly overlapping, around the edge of the dish. Cover and cook on high for 45 minutes or until well risen. Lift the pot out of the housing using oven mitts, brush the tops of the biscuits with the remaining egg, and brown under a broiler, if liked.

For cheat's mushroom pie, make up the mushroom casserole as above, but omit the stock and biscuit topping. Unroll one pastry sheet from a 14 oz package of 2 and trim the edges to make an oval shape. Transfer to an oiled baking sheet, brush with beaten egg and bake in a preheated oven at 400°F for 15–20 minutes or until golden. Cut into wedge shapes and serve on top of the casserole.

green bean risotto with pesto

Preparation time **20 minutes**
Cooking temperature **low**
Cooking time **2 hours**
   5 minutes–2½ hours
Serves **4**

2 tablespoons **butter**
1 tablespoon **olive oil**
1 **onion**, chopped
2 **garlic cloves**, chopped
1⅓ cups **Italian-style Arborio**
   or **risotto rice**
5 cups hot **vegetable stock**
2 teaspoons **pesto**
1 cup extra fine frozen **green**
   beans
generous ¾ cup frozen **peas**
salt and **black pepper**

To garnish
Parmesan shavings
basil leaves

Preheat the slow cooker, if necessary; see the manufacturer's instructions. Heat the butter and oil in a saucepan, add the onion, and fry, stirring, for 5 minutes or until softened and just beginning to brown.

Stir in the garlic and rice and cook for 1 minute. Add all but ⅔ cup of the stock, season with salt and pepper, then bring to the boil. Transfer to the slow cooker pot, cover with the lid, and cook on low for 1¾–2 hours.

Stir in the pesto and the remaining stock if more liquid is needed. Place the frozen vegetables on top of the rice, replace the lid, and cook for another 20–30 minutes or until the vegetables are hot. Serve, garnished with Parmesan shavings and basil leaves.

For green bean risotto with sage & pancetta,
add 3 oz diced pancetta or smoked fatty bacon when frying the chopped onion. Add 2 stems of sage to the mixture when adding the stock instead of the pesto. Replace the basil leaves with some tiny sage leaves.

warm beet & bean salad

Preparation time **25 minutes**
Cooking temperature **low**
Cooking time **3½–4½ hours**
Serves **4–5**

1 tablespoon **olive oil**
1 large **onion**, chopped
1 lb raw **beets**, peeled and
   finely diced
27 oz canned **borlotti beans**,
   rinsed and drained
2 cups **vegetable stock**
salt and **black pepper**

To serve
¼ **cucumber**, finely diced
1 cup **plain yogurt**
1 romaine or iceberg **lettuce**
4 red- or white-stemmed
   scallions, thinly sliced
¼ cup chopped fresh **cilantro**
   or **mint** leaves

Preheat the slow cooker, if necessary; see the manufacturer's instructions. Heat the oil in a skillet, add the onion, and fry, stirring, for 5 minutes or until pale golden. Add the beets to the pan with the drained beans, stock, and plenty of salt and black pepper. Bring to a boil, stirring.

Transfer the beet mixture to the slow cooker pot. Cover with the lid and cook on low for 3½–4½ hours or until the beets are tender. Stir well and lift the pot out of the cooker.

Stir the cucumber into the yogurt and season with salt and black pepper. Arrange the lettuce leaves on 4–5 individual plates. Top with the warm beet salad, then add spoonfuls of the cucumber yogurt. Scatter the scallions and cilantro or mint over the top and serve at once.

For warm beet salad with feta & tomatoes, prepare the salad as above. Mix 4 oz crumbled feta cheese with 2 diced tomatoes. Core, seed and dice ½ red or orange bell pepper and combine with the cheese and tomatoes. Add 4 tablespoons chopped mint and ¼ cup olive oil. Spoon over the warm salad and top with 3 cups arugula leaves.

sweet potato & egg curry

Preparation time **15 minutes**
Cooking temperature **low**
Cooking time **6–8 hours**
Serves **4**

1 tablespoon **sunflower oil**
1 **onion**, chopped
1 teaspoon **cumin seeds**,
  roughly crushed
1 teaspoon **ground coriander**
1 teaspoon **turmeric**
1 teaspoon **garam masala**
½ teaspoon **crushed dried
  red chilies**
2¼ cups diced **sweet
  potatoes**,
2 **garlic cloves**, finely
  chopped
13 oz canned **chopped
  tomatoes**
13½ oz canned **lentils**, drained
1¼ cups **vegetable stock**
1 teaspoon **superfine sugar**
6 **eggs**
1 cup frozen **peas**
⅔ cup **heavy cream**
small bunch of **cilantro**, torn
  into pieces
salt and **black pepper**

Preheat the slow cooker, if necessary; see the manufacturer's instructions. Heat the oil in a skillet, add the onion, and fry, stirring, for 5 minutes or until softened and just beginning to turn golden.

Stir in the spices, dried chilies, sweet potatoes, and garlic and fry for 2 minutes. Add the tomatoes, lentils, stock, and sugar and season with a little salt and black pepper. Bring to a boil, stirring. Spoon into the slow cooker pot, cover with the lid, and cook on low for 6–8 hours.

When almost ready to serve, put the eggs in a small saucepan, cover with cold water, and bring to a boil, then simmer for 8 minutes. Drain, crack the shells, and cool under cold running water. Peel and halve, then add to the slow cooker pot with the peas, cream, and half the cilantro. Cover and cook on low for 15 minutes.

Spoon into bowls, garnish with the remaining cilantro, and serve with rice or warmed naan, if liked.

For sweet potato & paneer curry, make up the curry as above, adding 13 oz diced paneer (Indian cheese) instead of the boiled eggs, reducing the peas to ⅔ cup and adding 8 baby corn cobs, halved if large.

mushroom & chestnut pie

Preparation time **45 minutes**
Cooking temperature **high**
Cooking time **5–6 hours**
Serves **4**

Sauce
1 tablespoon **butter**
1 tablespoon **sunflower oil**
1 **onion**, thinly sliced
1 tablespoon **all-purpose flour**
1¼ cups **vegetable stock**
⅓ cup **ruby Port**
1 teaspoon **Dijon mustard**
1 teaspoon **tomato paste**
salt and **black pepper**

Pastry dough
2⅓ cups **self-rising flour**
½ teaspoon **salt**
¾ cup **vegetable shortening**
2 tablespoons finely chopped **rosemary** leaves
about 1 cup **water**

Filling
1 large **flat mushroom**, sliced
2 cups sliced **cremini mushrooms**
7 oz vacuum-packed whole, peeled **chestnuts**

Preheat the slow cooker, if necessary; see the manufacturer's instructions. Make the sauce. Heat the butter and oil in a large skillet, add the onion, and fry for 5 minutes. Stir in the flour, then mix in the stock, port, mustard, and tomato paste. Season with salt and black pepper, bring to a boil, stirring, then take off the heat.

Make the pastry dough. Mix together the flour, salt, shortening, and rosemary. Gradually add enough cold water to mix to a soft but not sticky dough. Knead lightly, then roll out on a floured surface to a circle 13 inches across. Cut a quarter segment from the dough and reserve.

Lift the remaining dough into an oiled 2¼ quart ovenproof bowl and bring the cut edges together, overlapping them slightly so that the bowl is completely lined with dough, then press them together to seal. Layer the sauce, mushrooms, and chestnuts into the bowl, finishing with the sauce.

Pat the reserved dough into a circle the same size as the top of the bowl. Dampen the edges of the dough in the bowl with water and press the lid in place. Cover with oiled foil and dome the foil slightly. Tie in place with kitchen twine, then put into the slow cooker pot.

Pour boiling water into the slow cooker pot so that it comes halfway up the sides of the bowl. Cover and cook on high for 5–6 hours.

For rosemary pie with shallots & Madeira, make the sauce as above with 1 finely chopped onion and add ⅓ cup Madeira instead of the Port. Replace the peeled chestnuts with shallots. Continue as above.

spinach & zucchini tian

Preparation time **20 minutes**
Cooking temperature **high**
Cooking time **1½–2 hours**
Serves **4**

¼ cup **long-grain rice**
butter for greasing
1 **tomato**, sliced
1 tablespoon **olive oil**
½ **onion**, chopped
1 **garlic clove**, finely chopped
1 **zucchini**, about 6 oz,
  coarsely grated
4 cups thickly shredded
  spinach
3 **eggs**
⅛ cup **milk**
pinch of grated **nutmeg**
¼ cup chopped **mint**
salt and **black pepper**

Preheat the slow cooker, if necessary; see the manufacturer's instructions. Bring a small saucepan of water to a boil, add the rice, bring back to a boil, then simmer for 8–10 minutes or until tender. Meanwhile, butter the inside of a soufflé dish that is 5½ inches across the base and 3½ inches high. Line the bottom with nonstick parchment paper, and arrange tomato slices, overlapping, on top.

Heat the oil in a skillet, add the onion, and fry, stirring, for 5 minutes or until softened and just beginning to turn golden. Stir in the garlic, then add the zucchini and spinach, and cook for 2 minutes or until the spinach is just wilted.

Beat together the eggs, milk, nutmeg, and a little salt and black pepper. Drain the rice and stir into the spinach mixture with the egg mixture and mint. Mix well, then spoon into the dish. Cover loosely with buttered foil and lower into the slow cooker pot with foil straps (see page 15) or tie kitchen twine around the top edge.

Pour boiling water into the slow cooker pot to come halfway up the sides of the dish. Cover and cook on high for 1½–2 hours or until the tian is set in the middle. Lift out of the slow cooker, let stand for 5 minutes, then remove the foil, loosen the edge, and turn out onto a plate. Cut into wedges and serve warm with salad, if liked.

For cheesy spinach & pine nut tian, omit the zucchini and instead stir in ½ cup freshly grated Parmesan cheese, a small bunch of chopped basil, and ¼ cup toasted pine nuts.

dum aloo

Preparation time **15 minutes**
Cooking temperature **high**
Cooking time **6¼–7¼ hours**
Serves **4**

2 tablespoons **sunflower oil**
1 large **onion**, sliced
1 teaspoon **cumin seeds**,
crushed
4 **cardamom pods**, crushed
1 teaspoon **black onion
seeds** (optional)
1 teaspoon **ground turmeric**
½ teaspoon **ground cinnamon**
1 inch **fresh ginger**, peeled
and finely chopped
13 oz canned **chopped
tomatoes**
1¼ cups **vegetable stock**
1 teaspoon **superfine sugar**
1½ lb **new potatoes**
3 cups baby **leaf spinach**
salt and **black pepper**
cilantro leaves, to garnish
warm **naan**, to serve

Preheat the slow cooker, if necessary; see the manufacturer's instructions. Heat the oil in a large skillet, add the onion and fry, stirring, for 5 minutes or until lightly browned.

Mix in the cumin seeds, cardamom pods and seeds, onion seeds (if used), ground spices, and ginger. Cook for 1 minute, then mix in the tomatoes, stock, sugar, and season with salt and black pepper. Bring to a boil, stirring.

Cut the potatoes into thick slices or halves (if they are small) so that all the pieces are of a similar size. Transfer to the slow cooker pot and pour the sauce over the top. Cover and cook on high for 6–7 hours or until the potatoes are tender.

Add the spinach and cook, still on high, for another 15 minutes until it is just wilted. Stir the curry and serve sprinkled with torn cilantro leaves and accompanied with warm naan and a lentil dhal and plain rice, if liked.

For dum aloo with saffron & chickpeas (garbanzo beans), add 2 large pinches of saffron threads instead of the turmeric and mix into the pan when you add the tomatoes. Reduce the amount of potatoes to 1 lb. Drain 13½ oz canned chickpeas (garbanzo beans) and stir into the mixture. Pour over the hot sauce and cook as above.

moroccan seven-vegetable stew

Preparation time **25 minutes**
Cooking temperature **low** and **high**
Cooking time **6¼ hours–8 hours 20 minutes**
Serves **4**

2 tablespoons **olive oil**
1 large **onion**, chopped
2 **carrots**, diced
2½ cups diced **rutabaga**
1 **red bell pepper**, cored, seeded, and chopped
3 **garlic cloves**, finely chopped
1¼ cups frozen **fava beans**
13 oz canned **chopped tomatoes**
3 teaspoons **harissa** (Moroccan chili paste)
1 teaspoon **ground turmeric**
¾ inch **fresh ginger**, peeled and finely chopped
1 cup **vegetable stock**
10 **okra pods**, thickly sliced
salt and **black pepper**
mint leaves, torn, to garnish

Preheat the slow cooker, if necessary; see the manufacturer's instructions. Heat the oil in a large skillet, add the onion, and fry, stirring, for 5 minutes or until lightly browned.

Add the carrots and rutabaga to skillet with the red bell pepper, garlic, beans, and tomatoes. Mix in the harissa, turmeric, and ginger, then pour on the stock and season with salt and black pepper. Bring to a boil, stirring.

Spoon the mixture into the slow cooker pot and press the vegetables beneath the surface of the stock. Cover and cook on low for 6–8 hours or until the root vegetables are tender.

Stir in the okra, cover, and cook on high for 15–20 minutes or until the okra are tender but still bright green. Garnish with mint leaves and serve with couscous soaked in boiling water and flavored with olive oil, lemon juice, and golden raisins.

For Moroccan beef & vegetable stew, fry the onion with 10 oz ground beef, then add just 1 chopped carrot and 1 cup diced rutabaga, the red bell pepper, garlic, ¾ cup frozen fava beans, and the chopped tomatoes. Add the remaining ingredients and cook in the slow cooker for 8–10 hours. Add the okra and finish as above.

ratatouille with ricotta dumplings

Preparation time **25 minutes**
Cooking temperature **high**
Cooking time **3¼–4 hours
20 minutes**
Serves **4**

3 tablespoons **olive oil**
1 **onion**, chopped
1 **eggplant**, sliced
2 **zucchini**, about 12 oz in
total, sliced
1 **red bell pepper**, cored,
seeded, and cubed
1 **yellow bell pepper**, cored,
seeded, and cubed
2 **garlic cloves**, finely
chopped
1 tablespoon **all-purpose
flour**
13 oz canned **chopped
tomatoes**
1¼ cups **vegetable stock**
2–3 stems of **rosemary**
salt and **black pepper**

Dumplings
¾ cup **all-purpose flour**
3 oz **ricotta cheese**
grated rind of ½ **lemon**
1 **egg**, beaten

Preheat the slow cooker, if necessary; see the manufacturer's instructions. Heat the oil in a skillet, add the onion and eggplant, and fry, stirring, for 5 minutes or until softened and just beginning to turn golden.

Stir in the zucchini, bell peppers, and garlic and fry for 3–4 minutes. Mix in the flour, then the tomatoes, stock, rosemary, and a little salt and black pepper. Bring to a boil, then spoon into the slow cooker pot. Cover and cook on high for 3–4, hours until the vegetables are tender.

When almost ready to serve, make the dumplings. Put the flour, ricotta, lemon rind, and a little salt and black pepper into a bowl. Add the egg and mix to a soft but not sticky dough. Cut into 12 pieces and roll each piece into a ball with floured hands.

Stir the ratatouille and arrange the dumplings on the top. Replace the lid and cook for 15–20 minutes or until light and firm to the touch. Spoon into bowls and eat with a spoon and fork.

For chakchouka, make up the ratatouille as above and, when cooked, make 4 depressions in the vegetables with a spoon. Break an egg into each depression, then cover the slow cooker pot and cook on high for 10–15 minutes or until the eggs are just set. Spoon into shallow dishes to serve.

mixed mushroom & lentil braise

Preparation time **25 minutes**
Cooking temperature **low**
Cooking time **6–8 hours**
Serves **4**

2 tablespoons **olive oil**, plus
  extra to serve
1 large **onion**, chopped
3 **garlic cloves**, chopped
13 oz canned **chopped
  tomatoes**
1¼ cups **vegetable stock**
⅔ cup **red wine** (or extra
  stock)
1 tablespoon **tomato paste**
2 teaspoons **superfine sugar**
⅔ cup **Puy or green lentils**
12 oz **cup mushrooms**,
  halved or quartered
4 oz **shiitake mushrooms**,
  halved if large
4 large **field mushrooms**,
  about 8 oz in total
salt and **black pepper**

To serve
arugula leaves
Parmesan cheese shavings
fried rounds of **polenta**

Preheat the slow cooker, if necessary; see the manufacturer's instructions. Heat the oil in a large skillet, add the onion, and fry, stirring, for 5 minutes or until lightly browned. Mix in the garlic, tomatoes, stock, wine (if used), tomato paste, and sugar, and season with salt and black pepper. Add the Puy lentils and bring to a boil.

Put the mushrooms in the slow cooker pot and pour over the lentil mixture, then cover and cook on low for 6–8 hours, stirring once, if possible.

Serve with arugula leaves tossed with Parmesan shavings and a drizzle of olive oil and fried rounds of polenta.

For mixed mushroom & lentil cheesy bake, make and cook the mushroom and lentil mixture as above. Mix together 3 eggs, 1 cup plain yogurt, 3 oz crumbled feta cheese, and a pinch of grated nutmeg. Press the cooked mushroom mixture into an even layer, then spoon the yogurt mix on top. Arrange 2 sliced tomatoes on top and cook on high for 45 minutes–1¼ hours, until the topping is set. Lift the pot out of the housing using oven mitts and brown under a hot broiler, if liked.

pumpkin & parmesan gnocchi

Preparation time **20 minutes**
Cooking temperature **low**
Cooking time **6–8 hours**
Serves **4**

1 tablespoon **olive oil**
2 tablespoons **butter**
1 **onion**, thinly sliced
2 **garlic cloves**, finely
   chopped
2 tablespoons **all-purpose
   flour**
⅔ cup dry **white wine**
1¼ cups **vegetable stock**
2–3 stems of **sage**, plus extra
   to garnish (optional)
3 cups diced **pumpkin** (or
   butternut squash flesh)
1 lb chilled **gnocchi**
½ cup **heavy cream**
freshly grated **Parmesan
   cheese**
salt and **black pepper**

Preheat the slow cooker, if necessary; see the
manufacturer's instructions. Heat the oil and butter
in a skillet, add the onion, and fry, stirring, for 5 minutes
or until just beginning to turn golden.

Stir in the garlic, cook for 2 minutes, then stir in the
flour. Gradually mix in the wine and stock and heat,
stirring until smooth. Add the sage and season well.

Add the pumpkin to the slow cooker pot, pour over the
hot sauce, then press the pumpkin beneath the surface
of the liquid. Cover with the lid and cook on low for
6–8 hours or until the pumpkin is tender.

When almost ready to serve, bring a large saucepan of
water to a boil, add the gnocchi, bring the water back
to a boil, and cook for 2–3 minutes or until the gnocchi
float to the surface and are piping hot. Pour into a
colander to drain.

Stir the cream, then the gnocchi, into the pumpkin,
mix together lightly, then spoon into shallow bowls and
serve topped with grated Parmesan and a few extra
sage leaves, if liked.

For pumpkin pasta with dolcelatte, make up the
pumpkin mixture as above, then cook 8 oz rigatoni
or penne pasta in a saucepan of boiling water for
10 minutes or until tender. Drain. Stir the cream into
the pumpkin mixture as above, then stir in the pasta
instead of the gnocchi and top with 4 oz diced
dolcelatte (or Gorgonzola dolce) cheese instead
of the Parmesan.

hot pickled beets

Preparation time **15 minutes**
Cooking temperature **low**
Cooking time **6–8 hours**
Serves **4**

1 tablespoon **olive oil**
2 **red onions**, roughly
  chopped
1 bunch of **beets**, about 1 lb
  in total, trimmed, peeled, and
  cut into ½ inch cubes
1 red-skinned **apple**, cored
  and diced
1½ inch **fresh ginger**, peeled
  and finely chopped
¼ cup **red wine vinegar**
2 tablespoons **honey**
2 cups **vegetable stock**
salt and **black pepper**

To garnish
sour cream
dill

Preheat the slow cooker, if necessary; see the manufacturer's instructions. Heat the oil in a skillet, add the onions, and fry, stirring, for 5 minutes or until just beginning to soften and turn golden.

Stir in the beets and cook for 3 minutes, then add the apple, ginger, vinegar, and honey. Pour in the stock, add a little salt and black pepper and bring to a boil. Pour the mixture into the slow cooker pot, press the beets below the surface of the liquid, then cover and cook on low for 6–8 hours until tender.

Serve hot as an appetizer topped with spoonfuls of sour cream and chopped dill or as a vegetable side dish with roast pork or beef or cold with cold sliced meats.

For hot beets with orange & caraway, make up the recipe as above but omit the ginger and vinegar, and instead add the grated rind and juice of 1 orange and 1½ teaspoons caraway seeds. Serve topped with spoonfuls of sour cream, a little paprika, and some orange rind curls.

tarka dahl

Preparation time **15 minutes**
Cooking temperature **high**
Cooking time **3–4 hours**
Serves **4**

1⅓ cups **red lentils**
1 **onion**, finely chopped
½ teaspoon **turmeric**
½ teaspoon **cumin seeds**,
  roughly crushed
¾ inch **fresh ginger**, peeled
  and finely chopped
7 oz canned **chopped
  tomatoes**
2½ cups boiling **vegetable
  stock**
salt and **black pepper**
⅔ cup **plain yogurt**
cilantro leaves, torn,
  to garnish
warm **naan**, to serve

Tarka
1 tablespoon **sunflower oil**
2 teaspoons **black mustard
  seeds**
½ teaspoon **cumin seeds**,
  roughly crushed
pinch of **turmeric**
2 **garlic cloves**, finely
  chopped

Preheat the slow cooker, if necessary; see the
manufacturer's instructions. Rinse the lentils well with
cold water, drain, and put into the slow cooker pot with
the onion, spices, ginger, tomatoes and boiling stock.

Stir in a little salt and black pepper, cover with the lid,
and cook on high for 3–4 hours or until the lentils are
soft and tender.

When almost ready to serve, make the tarka. Heat
the oil in a small skillet, add the remaining tarka
ingredients, and fry, stirring, for 2 minutes. Roughly
mash the lentil mixture, then spoon into bowls, add
spoonfuls of yogurt, and drizzle with the tarka. Sprinkle
with cilantro leaves and serve with warm naan.

For tarka dahl with spinach, cook the lentils in
the same way as above, adding 4 cups washed
and roughly shredded spinach leaves for the last
15 minutes. Fry the tarka spices as above, adding
¼ teaspoon crushed dried red chili seeds, if liked.

spanish potatoes

Preparation time **15 minutes**
Cooking temperature **high**
Cooking time **4–5 hours**
Serves **4**

2 tablespoons **olive oil**
1 large **red onion**, thinly sliced
2 **garlic cloves**, finely
   chopped
1 teaspoon **smoked paprika**
¼–½ teaspoon crushed dried
   red chilies (to taste)
1 **red bell pepper**, cored,
   seeded, and diced
1 **yellow bell pepper**, cored,
   seeded, and diced
13 oz canned **chopped
   tomatoes**
1¼ cups **vegetable stock**
2–3 stems of **thyme**
8 pitted **dry olives**
2 large (1¼ lb) **baking
   potatoes**, cut into 1 inch
   chunks
salt and **black pepper**
crusty bread, to serve

Preheat the slow cooker, if necessary; see the manufacturer's instructions. Heat the oil in a skillet, add the onion, and fry, stirring, for 5 minutes or until just beginning to turn golden.

Stir in the garlic, paprika, dried chilies and bell peppers, and cook for 2 minutes. Mix in the tomatoes, stock, thyme, olives, and some salt and black pepper, then bring to a boil.

Add the potatoes to the slow cooker pot, pour over the hot tomato mixture, cover with the lid, and cook on high for 4–5 hours or until the potatoes are tender. Serve with warm crusty bread and a dressed green salad, if liked.

For Spanish sweet potatoes, make up the recipe as above, using sweet potatoes instead of baking potatoes and omitting the olives. Cook on high for 3–4 hours and serve in bowls topped with spoonfuls of Greek yogurt and torn cilantro leaves.

braised celery with orange

Preparation time **10 minutes**
Cooking temperature **high**
Cooking time **4–5 hours**
Serves **4–6**

2 **celery hearts**
grated rind and juice of
    1 small **orange**
2 tablespoons **light brown
    sugar**
13 oz canned **chopped
    tomatoes**
salt and **black pepper**

Preheat the slow cooker, if necessary; see the manufacturer's instructions. Cut each celery heart in half lengthwise, then rinse under cold water to remove any traces of dirt. Drain and put into the slow cooker pot.

Mix the remaining ingredients together and pour over the celery. Cover with the lid and cook on high for 4–5 hours or until the celery is tender. If you would prefer a thicker sauce, pour off the liquid from the slow cooker pot into a saucepan and boil rapidly for 4–5 minutes to reduce. Pour back over the celery and serve as an accompaniment to roast chicken, pork, or duck.

For braised fennel with orange, cut 3 small fennel bulbs into halves, add to the slow cooker pot with the remaining ingredients, and cook as above. Sprinkle the top with pieces torn from one-quarter of a ciabatta bread fried in 2 tablespoons olive oil until crisp and golden.

nut & apricot pilaf

Preparation time **25 minutes**
Cooking temperature **low**
Cooking time **3–3½ hours**
Serves **4**

1 tablespoon **olive oil**
1 large **onion**, chopped
½ cup mixed **pistachios,
    walnuts**, and **hazelnuts**
3 tablespoons **sunflower
    seeds**
1 cup instant **brown rice**
4¼ cups **vegetable stock**
⅓ cup chopped dried **apricots**
3 tablespoons **currants**
1 **cinnamon stick**, halved
6 **cloves**
3 **bay leaves**
1 tablespoon **tomato paste**
salt and **black pepper**
lightly toasted **mixed nuts**,
    to garnish

Preheat the slow cooker, if necessary; see the manufacturer's instructions. Heat the oil in a skillet, add the onion and fry, stirring, for 5 minutes or until lightly browned.

Add the nuts and seeds and fry until lightly browned. Stir in the rice and stock, followed by the dried fruit, spices, bay leaves, and tomato paste, then season with salt and black pepper to taste. Bring to a boil, stirring.

Transfer the mixture to the slow cooker pot. Cover with the lid and cook on low for 3–3½ hours or until the rice is tender and the stock has been absorbed. Discard the cinnamon, cloves, and bay leaves before serving, garnished with extra nuts.

For eggplant & apricot pilaf, heat 3 tablespoons olive oil, add the onion and 1 sliced eggplant, and fry until lightly browned. Continue as above, replacing the hazelnuts with almonds and adding the sunflower seeds, the rice, stock, and just ¼ cup of the apricots plus ⅓ cup chopped, pitted dates. Add the remaining ingredients and continue as above.

desserts, drinks, & preserves

sticky rum bananas with vanilla

Preparation time **10 minutes**
Cooking temperature **low**
Cooking time **1½–2 hours**
Serves **4**

2 tablespoons **butter**
⅓ cup **light brown sugar**
grated rind and juice of **1 lime**
1 **vanilla bean** or 1 teaspoon
   vanilla extract
3 tablespoons **white** or **dark
   rum**
1 cup boiling **water**
6 small **bananas**, peeled and
   halved lengthwise
curls of **lime rind**, to decorate

Preheat the slow cooker, if necessary; see the manufacturer's instructions. Add the butter, sugar, and lime rind and juice to the warming slow cooker pot and stir until the butter has melted.

Slit the vanilla bean along its length, open it out with a small sharp knife, and scrape the tiny black seeds away from inside the bean. Add the seeds and the bean or vanilla extract, if using, to the slow cooker pot along with the rum and boiling water.

Add the bananas to the slow cooker pot, arranging them in a single layer and pressing them beneath the liquid as much as you can. Cover with the lid and cook on low for 1½–2 hours or until the bananas are hot.

Spoon the bananas and rum sauce into dishes and decorate with extra lime rind curls and scoops of vanilla ice cream, if liked.

For sticky brandied pineapple, make up the vanilla syrup as above, replacing the rum with brandy. Trim the top off a medium pineapple, cut away the skin and eyes, and slice, then halve each slice, cutting away the core. Add to the syrup and press beneath the syrup. Cover and cook as above.

crème caramels

Preparation time **20 minutes**, plus chilling
Cooking temperature **low**
Cooking time **2½–3½ hours**
Serves **4**

butter, for greasing
⅔ cup **granulated sugar**
½ cup **water**
2 tablespoons boiling **water**
2 **eggs**
3 **egg yolks**
13 oz can **condensed milk**
½ cup **low-fat milk**
grated rind of ½ small **lemon**

Preheat the slow cooker, if necessary; see the manufacturer's instructions. Lightly butter 4 metal individual custard cups, each 1 cup. Pour the sugar and water into a small saucepan and heat gently, stirring occasionally until the sugar has completely dissolved.

Increase the heat and boil the syrup for 5 minutes, without stirring, until the syrup has turned golden, keeping a watchful eye as it cooks. Take the pan off the heat, add the boiling water and stand well back. Tilt the pan to mix, and when bubbles have subsided pour into the custard cups, tilting them so that the syrup coats the bottom and sides.

Put the eggs and egg yolks into a bowl and fork together. Pour the condensed milk and fresh milk into a saucepan, bring to a boil, then gradually beat into the egg mixture until smooth. Strain back into the pan, then stir in the lemon rind.

Pour the custard into the syrup-lined custard cups, then transfer the cups into the slow cooker pot. Cover the top of each one with a square of foil. Pour hot water around the cups so that the water comes halfway up the sides, then cover with the lid and cook on low for 2½–3½ hours or until the custard is set with just a slight wobble in the center. Lift out of the slow cooker pot with a dish towel, cool, then transfer to the refrigerator for 3–4 hours or overnight to chill.

Dip the bottom of the custard cups into boiling water for 10 seconds, loosen the top of the custard with a fingertip, then turn out onto rimmed plates.

saffron pears with chocolate

Preparation time **20 minutes**
Cooking temperature **low**
Cooking time **3–4 hours**
Serves **4**

1 ¼ cups **apple cider** or **apple juice**
3 tablespoons **superfine sugar**
large pinch of **saffron threads**
4 **cardamom pods**, roughly crushed
4 firm, ripe **pears**

Chocolate sauce
¼ cup **chocolate and hazelnut spread**
2 tablespoons **heavy cream**
2 tablespoons **milk**

Preheat the slow cooker, if necessary; see the manufacturer's instructions. Pour the apple cider or juice into a small saucepan, add the sugar, saffron, and cardamom pods and their tiny black seeds. Bring to a boil, then pour into the slow cooker pot.

Cut each pear in half lengthwise, leaving the stalk on, then cut away the skin. Remove the pear cores with a melon baller, if you have one, or a teaspoon. Add the pears to the slow cooker pot, pressing them beneath the surface of the liquid as much as you can. Cover with the lid and cook on low for 3–4 hours or until the pears are tender and pale yellow.

When ready to serve, put all the ingredients for the sauce into a small saucepan and warm together, stirring until smooth. Spoon the pears and some of the saffron sauce into shallow dishes, pour the chocolate sauce into a small pitcher, and let dinner guests drizzle the sauce over the pears just before eating. Complete with a spoonful of ice cream or crème fraîche, if liked.

For spiced pears with red wine, warm ⅔ cup red wine with ⅔ cup water, ¼ cup superfine sugar, the pared rind of ½ small orange, 1 small cinnamon stick, halved, and 4 cloves. Pour into the slow cooker pot, add 4 halved, peeled, and cored pears, then cover and cook as above. Serve with spoonfuls of crème fraîche or ice cream.

lemon custard creams

Preparation time **15 minutes**,
   plus chilling
Cooking temperature **low**
Cooking time **2–2½ hours**
Serves **6**

2 **eggs**
3 **egg yolks**
½ cup **superfine sugar**
grated rind of 2 **lemons** and
   the juice of 1 **lemon**
1¼ cups **heavy cream**
1 cup **blueberries**,
   to serve

Preheat the slow cooker, if necessary; see the manufacturer's instructions. Put the eggs and egg yolks, sugar, and lemon rind into a bowl and beat together until just mixed.

Pour the cream into a small saucepan, bring just to a boil, then gradually beat into the egg mixture. Strain the lemon juice and gradually beat into the cream mixture.

Pour the mixture into 6 small coffee cups and put them in the slow cooker pot. Pour hot water into the pot so that it comes halfway up the sides of the cups. Loosely cover the tops of the cups with a piece of foil, cover, and cook on low for 2–2½ hours or until the custards are just set.

Lift the cups carefully out of the slow cooker with a dish towel and let cool. Transfer to the refrigerator to chill for 3–4 hours or overnight.

Set the cups on their saucers and decorate the tops of the custard with blueberries.

For lime & elderflower custard creams, make the desserts as above but with the grated rind and juice of 2 limes and 2 tablespoons undiluted elderflower syrup instead of the lemon rind and juice. Cook in coffee cups, then serve chilled with fresh strawberries drizzled with a little extra elderflower syrup.

chocolate brownie puddings

Preparation time **20 minutes**
Cooking temperature **high**
Cooking time **1¼–1½ hours**
Serves **4**

4 oz plain **dark chocolate**,
   plus 8 extra small squares
6 tablespoons **butter**
2 **eggs**
2 **egg yolks**
⅓ cup **superfine sugar**
½ teaspoon **vanilla extract**
⅓ cup **all-purpose flour**

To decorate
sifted **confectioners' sugar**
mini pastel-colored
   marshmallows
vanilla ice cream or **crème
   fraîche**

Preheat the slow cooker if necessary; see the manufacturer's instructions. Break the 4 oz chocolate into pieces, put into a saucepan with the butter, and heat gently, stirring occasionally, until melted. Take off the heat and set aside.

Beat together the whole eggs, egg yolks, sugar, and vanilla extract in a large bowl with an electric mixer for 3–4 minutes or until light and frothy. Gradually beat in the melted chocolate mixture.

Sift the flour into the chocolate mix and fold together. Pour into 4 individual metal cup molds that have been buttered and the bottoms lined with parchment paper. Press 2 squares of chocolate into the center of each, then loosely cover the tops with squares of buttered foil.

Transfer the metal molds to the slow cooker pot and pour boiling water into the pot to come halfway up the sides of the molds. Cover with the lid and cook on high for 1¼–1½ hours, until well risen and the tops spring back when lightly pressed.

Loosen the puddings with a knife, turn out into shallow serving dishes and remove the lining paper. Sprinkle with sifted confectioners' sugar. Serve with marshmallows, spoonfuls of vanilla ice cream, or crème fraîche.

For brandied cherry brownie puddings, soak 8 drained, canned pitted black cherries in 1 tablespoon of brandy for at least 2 hours, longer if possible. Make up the brownie mixture as above and drop 2 cherries into the centers of each instead of the square of chocolate.

plum & polenta cake

Preparation time **30 minutes**
Cooking temperature **high**
Cooking time **3–3½ hours**
Serves **6**

10 tablespoons (1¼ sticks)
   butter, at room temperature,
   plus extra for greasing
7 oz sweet red **plums**, pitted
   and halved
¾ cup **superfine sugar**
2 **eggs**, beaten
1 cup **ground almonds**
¼ cup fine **polenta** (cornmeal)
½ teaspoon **baking powder**
grated rind and juice of
   ½ **orange**

To decorate
2 tablespoons toasted
   slivered almonds
sifted **confectioners' sugar**

Preheat the slow cooker, if necessary; see the manufacturer's instructions. Butter a 5 cup oval or round heatproof dish that will fit comfortably in your slow cooker pot and line the bottom with a piece of wax paper. Arrange the plum halves, cut side down, in rings in the bottom of the dish.

Cream together the measured butter and sugar in a mixing bowl until light and fluffy. Gradually beat the eggs and ground almonds alternately into the mixture. Stir in the polenta, baking powder, and orange rind and juice and beat until smooth.

Spoon the mixture over the plums and smooth with a knife. Cover the dish with buttered foil, then stand it on an upturned saucer or 2 individual flan rings in the slow cooker pot. Pour boiling water into the pot to come halfway up the sides of the dish. Cover and cook on high for 3–3½ hours or until the top of the cake is dry and springs back when pressed with a fingertip.

Remove the dish carefully from the slow cooker using a dish towel. Take off the foil and let cool slightly. Run a knife around the inside edge of the dish to loosen the cake and turn it out onto a serving plate. Remove the lining paper, sprinkle the top with toasted, slivered almonds, and dust with a little sifted confectioners' sugar to decorate. Cut into wedges and serve warm or cold with spoonfuls of whipped cream, if liked.

For apple & polenta cake, follow the recipe as above, but replace the plums with 2 Braeburn apples, peeled, cored, and thickly sliced and tossed with the grated rind and juice of ½ lemon.

pineapple upside-down puddings

Preparation time **20 minutes**
Cooking temperature **high**
Cooking time **2–2½ hours**
Serves **4**

butter, for greasing
¼ cup **light corn syrup**
2 tablespoons **light brown sugar**
7½ oz canned **pineapple rings**, drained and chopped
3 tablespoons roughly chopped **candied cherries**

Sponge
4 tablespoons **butter**, at room temperature, or soft margarine
¼ cup **superfine sugar**
⅓ cup **self-rising flour**
¼ cup **dried shredded coconut**
1 **egg**
1 tablespoon **milk**

Preheat the slow cooker if necessary; see the manufacturer's instructions. Lightly butter 4 metal individual cup molds, the bottoms lined with a circle of nonstick parchment paper. Add 1 tablespoon of corn syrup and ½ tablespoon sugar to the bottom of each, then add three-quarters of the pineapple and the cherries.

Make the sponge. Put all the ingredients plus the remaining pineapple into a bowl and beat together until smooth.

Spoon the mixture into the molds. Level the surface with the back of a small spoon, then cover the top of each mold loosely with buttered foil. Stand the molds in the slow cooker pot, then pour boiling water into the pot to come halfway up the sides of the molds. Cover with the lid and cook on high for 2–2½ hours or until the sponge is well risen and springs back when pressed with a fingertip.

Remove the foil, loosen the edges of the puddings with a round-bladed knife, and turn out into shallow bowls. Peel away the lining paper and serve with heavy cream, if liked.

For plum & almond puddings, add the syrup and sugar to the bottom of the molds as above, then add 4 pitted and sliced red plums instead of the pineapple and cherries. Make up the sponge as above, omitting the coconut and adding ¼ cup ground almonds and a few drops of almond extract.

chocolate bread & butter pudding

Preparation time **35 minutes**
Cooking temperature **low**
Cooking time **4–4½ hours**
Serves **4–5**

½ **French bread**, thinly sliced
4 tablespoons **butter**, at room
   temperature
3½ oz **white chocolate**,
   chopped
4 **egg yolks**
¼ cup **superfine sugar**, plus
   3 tablespoons extra for
   caramelizing
⅔ cup **heavy cream**
1¼ cups **milk**
1 teaspoon **vanilla extract**

Blueberry coulis
scant 1 cup **blueberries**
1 tablespoon **superfine sugar**
¼ cup **water**

To decorate
few extra **blueberries**
little **white chocolate**,
   chopped

Preheat the slow cooker, if necessary; see the manufacturer's instructions. Spread the slices of French bread with the butter. Layer the bread in a 5 cup heatproof bowl that will fit comfortably in your slow cooker pot, allowing for a gap of at least ¾ inch all the way around. Sprinkle the chopped white chocolate between the layers of bread.

Beat together the egg yolks and sugar in a bowl with a fork. Pour the cream and milk into a saucepan and bring just to a boil. Gradually stir into the egg mixture, then stir in the vanilla extract.

Pour the cream mixture over the layered bread slices and let stand for 10 minutes.

Cover the top of the dish with foil, then lower it into the slow cooker pot, using foil straps (see page 15). Pour hot water around the dish to come halfway up the sides, cover with the lid, and cook on low for 4–4½ hours or until the custard has set.

Meanwhile, make the blueberry coulis. Purée the blueberries with the sugar and water until smooth. Pour into a pitcher and set aside.

Lift the dish carefully out of the slow cooker. Remove the foil and sprinkle the remaining sugar over the top of the pudding. Caramelize the sugar under a hot broiler or with a cook's blowtorch. To serve, spoon the bread and butter pudding into bowls and sprinkle with extra blueberries and white chocolate. Stir the blueberry coulis and pour it around the pudding.

lemon & poppy seed drizzle cake

Preparation time **25 minutes**
Cooking temperature **high**
Cooking time **4½–5 hours**
Serves **6–8**

½ cup (1 stick) **butter**, at room
　temperature, plus extra
　for greasing
⅔ cup **superfine sugar**
2 **eggs**, beaten
1 cup **self-rising flour**
2 tablespoons **poppy seeds**
grated rind of 1 **lemon**
lemon rind curls, to decorate
crème fraîche (or an equal
　amount of whipping cream
　and sour cream mixed
　together), to serve

Lemon syrup
juice of 1½ **lemons**
⅔ cup **superfine sugar**

Preheat the slow cooker, if necessary; see the manufacturer's instructions. Lightly butter a soufflé dish that is 5½ inches across the bottom and 3½ inches high, and line the bottom with a circle of nonstick parchment paper.

Cream together the measured butter and sugar in a bowl with a wooden spoon or electric hand mixer. Gradually mix in alternate spoonfuls of beaten egg and flour, and continue adding and beating until the mixture is smooth. Stir in the poppy seeds and lemon rind, then spoon the mixture into the soufflé dish and spread the top level. Cover the top of the dish loosely with buttered foil and then lower into the slow cooker pot using foil straps (see page 15).

Pour boiling water into the slow cooker pot so that it comes halfway up the sides of the dish. Cover with the lid and cook on high for 4½–5 hours or until the cake is dry and springs back when pressed with a fingertip.

Lift the dish carefully out of the slow cooker, remove the foil, and loosen the edge of the cake with a knife. Turn out onto a plate or shallow dish with a rim. Quickly warm the lemon juice and sugar together for the syrup and as soon as the sugar has dissolved, pour the syrup over the cake. Let stand to cool and let the syrup soak in. Cut into slices and serve with spoonfuls of crème fraîche, decorated with lemon rind curls.

For citrus drizzle cake, omit the lemon rind and poppy seeds from the cake mixture and stir in the grated rind of ½ lemon, ½ lime, and ½ small orange. Bake as above. Make the syrup using the juice of the grated fruits and sugar.

sticky toffee apple pudding

Preparation time **30 minutes**
Cooking temperature **high**
Cooking time **3–3½ hours**
Serves **4–5**

4 tablespoons **butter**, diced,
  plus extra for greasing
1¼ cups **self-rising flour**
½ cup packed **brown sugar**
2 **eggs**
2 tablespoons **milk**
1 **apple**, cored and finely
  chopped
vanilla ice cream, **crème
  fraîche**, or **light cream**,
  to serve

Sauce
½ cup packed **dark sugar**
2 tablespoons **butter**, diced
1¼ cups boiling **water**

Preheat the slow cooker, if necessary; see the manufacturer's instructions. Butter the inside of a soufflé dish that is 5½ inches across and 3½ inches high. Put the flour in a bowl, add the measured butter, and rub in with the fingertips until the mixture resembles fine bread crumbs. Stir in the sugar, then mix in the eggs and milk until smooth. Stir in the apple.

Spoon the mixture into the soufflé dish and spread it level. Sprinkle the sugar for the sauce over the top and dot with the 2 tablespoons butter. Pour the measured boiling water over the top, then cover loosely with foil.

Lower the dish carefully into the slow cooker pot, using foil straps (see page 15). Pour boiling water into the pot so that it comes halfway up the sides of the soufflé dish. Cover and cook on high for 3–3½ hours or until the sponge is well risen and the sauce is bubbling around the edges.

Lift the dish out of the slow cooker. Remove the foil and loosen the sides of the sponge. Cover with a dish that is large enough to catch the sauce, then invert and remove the soufflé dish. Serve with spoonfuls of vanilla ice cream, crème fraîche, or light cream.

For sticky banana pudding, prepare the pudding as above but replace the chopped apple with 1 small, ripe and roughly mashed banana and ½ teaspoon ground cinnamon. Make up the sauce and cook as above.

iced jamaican ginger cake

Preparation time **25 minutes**
Cooking temperature **high**
Cooking time **4½–5 hours**
Serves **6**

7 tablespoons **butter**, plus extra for greasing
½ cup packed **dark brown sugar**
⅓ cup **light corn syrup**
⅔ cup chopped, pitted **dates**
¾ cup, plus 1 tablespoon **whole-wheat flour**
¾ cup **self-rising flour**
½ teaspoon **bicarbonate of soda**
2 teaspoons **ground ginger**
3 pieces of **preserved ginger**, drained of syrup, 2 chopped and 1 cut into strips
2 **eggs**, beaten
scant ½ cup **milk**
1 cup **confectioners' sugar**
3–3½ teaspoons **water**

Preheat the slow cooker, if necessary; see the manufacturer's instructions. Butter a soufflé dish that is 5½ inches across the bottom and 3½ inches high and line the bottom with a circle of nonstick parchment paper.

Put the measured butter, sugar, syrup, and dates into a saucepan and heat gently, stirring, until the butter and sugar have melted. Take the pan off the heat, add the flours, baking soda, ground and chopped ginger, eggs, and milk and beat until smooth. Pour into the lined dish and cover the top loosely with buttered foil.

Lower the dish carefully into the slow cooker pot on foil straps (see page 15) or tie kitchen twine around the top edge of the dish. Pour boiling water into the pot to come halfway up the sides of the dish, cover with the lid, and cook on high for 4½–5 hours or until a skewer comes out cleanly when inserted into the center of the ginger cake.

Take the dish out of the slow cooker pot, let stand for 10 minutes, then remove the foil and loosen the edge of the cake with a knife. Turn out onto a wire rack, peel off the lining paper, and let cool.

Sift the confectioners' sugar into a bowl and mix in just enough water to make a smooth, thick icing. Spoon over the top of the cake, then decorate with the strips of ginger. Let set. Cut into wedges to serve.

For banana ginger cake, omit the dates from the ginger cake, and add 1 small mashed banana mixed with 1 tablespoon lemon juice when adding the chopped ginger. Cook and ice as above.

cherry & chocolate puddings

Preparation time **25 minutes**
Cooking temperature **high**
Cooking time **1½–2 hours**
Serves **4**

4 tablespoons **butter**, plus
  extra for greasing
¼ cup **superfine sugar**
⅓ cup **self-rising flour**
1 **egg**
1 tablespoon **unsweetened
  cocoa powder**
¼ teaspoon **baking powder**
¼ teaspoon **ground cinnamon**
14 oz canned pitted **black
  cherries**, drained

Chocolate sauce
3½ oz **white chocolate**,
  broken into pieces
⅔ cup **heavy cream**

Preheat the slow cooker, if necessary; see the manufacturer's instructions. Butter the inside of 4 individual metal cup molds, each 1 cup, and line the bottom of each with a circle of wax paper.

Put the measured butter, sugar, flour, egg, cocoa, baking powder, and cinnamon in a bowl and beat them together with a wooden spoon until smooth.

Arrange 7 cherries in the bottom of each mold. Roughly chop the remainder and stir them into the pudding mix. Spoon the mixture into the molds and level the tops. Loosely cover the tops of the molds with foil and put them in the slow cooker pot. Pour boiling water into the pot so that it comes halfway up the sides of the molds, cover with the lid, and cook on high for 1½–2 hours or until the puddings are well risen and the tops spring back when pressed with a fingertip. Lift the puddings out of the slow cooker pot.

Make the sauce. Put the chocolate and cream in a small saucepan and heat gently, stirring occasionally, until melted. Loosen the edges of the puddings, turn them out into shallow bowls, peel away the lining paper, and pour the sauce around them before serving.

For cherry & almond puddings, prepare the sponge as above, omitting the cocoa and ground cinnamon and instead adding 2 tablespoons ground almonds and a few drops of almond extract. Cook as above, turn out, and serve with spoonfuls of vanilla ice cream.

dark chocolate & coffee pots

Preparation time **25 minutes**,
  plus chilling
Cooking temperature **low**
Cooking time **3–3½ hours**
Serves **4**

scant 2 cups **whole milk**
⅔ cup **heavy cream**
7 oz **dark chocolate**, broken
  into pieces
2 **eggs**
3 **egg yolks**
¼ cup **superfine sugar**
¼ teaspoon **ground cinnamon**
chocolate curls, to decorate

Topping
⅔ cup **heavy cream**
⅓ cup **coffee cream liqueur**

Preheat the slow cooker, if necessary; see the manufacturer's instructions. Pour the milk and cream into a saucepan and bring just to a boil. Remove from the heat, add the chocolate pieces, and set aside for 5 minutes, stirring occasionally, until the chocolate has melted.

Put the whole eggs, egg yolks, sugar, and cinnamon in a mixing bowl and beat until smooth. Gradually beat in the warm chocolate milk, then strain the mixture into 4 heatproof pots or mugs, each 8 fl oz.

Cover the tops of the pots or mugs with foil and stand them in the slow cooker pot. Pour hot water into the slow cooker pot to come halfway up the sides of the pots or mugs. Cover with the lid and cook on low for 3–3½ hours or until set.

Lift the dishes carefully out of the slow cooker pot using oven mitts. Let cool at room temperature, then transfer to the refrigerator for at least 4 hours until well chilled.

Just before serving, whip the cream for the topping until soft swirls form. Gradually beat in the liqueur, then spoon the flavored cream over the top of the desserts. Sprinkle with chocolate curls and serve.

For cappuccino pots with coffee cream liqueur, add 2 teaspoons instant coffee to the just-boiled cream and milk when adding the chocolate. Continue as above, but omit the cinnamon.

peaches with marsala & vanilla

Preparation time **15 minutes**

Cooking temperature **low** and **high**

Cooking time **1¼–1¾ hours**

Serves **4–6**

⅔ cup **marsala** or **sweet sherry**

⅔ cup **water**

⅓ cup **superfine sugar**

6 firm, ripe **peaches** or **nectarines**, halved and pits removed

1 **vanilla bean**, slit lengthwise

2 teaspoons **cornstarch**

1 cup **raspberries**

Preheat the slow cooker, if necessary; see the manufacturer's instructions. Put the marsala or sherry, the water, and sugar in a saucepan and bring to a boil.

Put the peach or nectarine halves and vanilla bean in the slow cooker pot and pour in the hot syrup. Cover with the lid and cook on low for 1–1½ hours or until hot and tender.

Lift the fruit out of the slow cooker pot and transfer to a serving dish. Remove the vanilla bean, then scrape the black seeds from the bean with a small sharp knife and stir the seeds back into the cooking syrup. Mix the cornstarch to a smooth paste with a little cold water, then stir into the cooking syrup and cook on high for 15 minutes, stirring occasionally.

Pour the thickened syrup over the fruit, sprinkle with the raspberries, and serve warm or chilled with spoonfuls of crème fraîche or vanilla ice cream, if liked.

For poached apples & pears with marsala & vanilla, make the marsala syrup as above. Peel, core, and quarter 3 Braeburn apples and 3 just-ripe pears. Add the fruit to the slow cooker pot with a slit vanilla bean and pour over the hot syrup. Cook and thicken the syrup as above.

christmas pudding

Preparation time **20 minutes**
Cooking temperature **high**
Cooking time **7–8 hours**
Reheating time **2–2½ hours**
Serves **6–8**

butter, for greasing
1½ lb mixed luxury **dried fruit**
   (with larger fruits diced)
⅓ cup roughly chopped
   pistachio nuts
1 tablespoon finely chopped
   candied or preserved **ginger**
1 **apple**, peeled, cored, and
   coarsely grated
grated rind and juice of
   1 **lemon**
grated rind and juice of
   1 **orange**
¼ cup **brandy**
¼ cup **dark brown sugar**
½ cup **self-rising flour**
¾ cup dried **bread crumbs**
   (or 1⅔ cups if fresh)
½ cup **vegetable shortening**
1 teaspoon **ground allspice**
2 **eggs**, beaten
¼ cup **brandy**, to serve
   (optional)

Preheat the slow cooker, if necessary; see the manufacturer's instructions. Check that a 1½ quart ovenproof bowl will fit inside your slow cooker pot with a little room to spare, then butter the inside of the bowl and line the bottom with a circle of nonstick parchment paper.

Put the dried fruit, nuts, ginger, and grated apple into a large bowl. Add the fruit rinds and juice and brandy and mix together well. Stir in the remaining ingredients. Spoon into the buttered bowl, pressing down well as you work. Cover with a large circle of nonstick parchment paper, then a piece of foil. Tie with kitchen twine and add a string handle.

Lower into the slow cooker pot, using foil straps (see page 15) and pour boiling water into the pot to come two-thirds up the sides of the bowl. Cover with the lid and cook on high for 7–8 hours. Check halfway through cooking and fill up with extra boiling water if needed. Take out of the slow cooker and let cool.

Cover with fresh foil, leaving the parchment paper in place. Retie with twine and keep in a cool place for 2 months or until Christmas.

When ready to serve, preheat the slow cooker, if needed, add the pudding, and boiling water as above, and reheat on high for 2–2½ hours. Remove the foil and paper, loosen the pudding, and turn out. Warm the brandy in a saucepan, if using. When it is just boiling, flame with a taper and quickly pour over the pudding. Serve with brandy butter or cream.

winter fruit compote

Preparation time **10 minutes**
Cooking temperature **low**
Cooking time **2½–3½ hours**
Serves **4**

3 cups **cranberries**
1 lb red **plums**, quartered
  and pitted
1⅓ cups halved red seedless
  grapes
4 teaspoons **cornstarch**
1¼ cups red **grape juice**
½ cup **superfine sugar**
1 **cinnamon stick**, halved
pared rind of 1 small **orange**

Lemon curd cream
⅔ cup **heavy cream**, lightly
  whipped
3 tablespoons **lemon curd**

Preheat the slow cooker, if necessary; see the manufacturer's instructions. Put the cranberries, plums, and grapes into the slow cooker pot.

Mix the cornstarch with a little of the grape juice in a bowl until smooth, then stir in the remaining juice. Pour into the slow cooker pot and add the sugar, cinnamon and orange rind. Stir together, then cover with the lid and cook on low for 2½–3½ hours or until the fruit is tender.

Stir, discard the cinnamon and orange rind, and serve warm or cold spooned into bowls and topped with the cream folded into the lemon curd.

For orchard fruit compote, follow the recipe as above, but replace the cranberries and grapes with 2 pears and 2 apples, peeled, cored, and thickly sliced.

baked apples with dates

Preparation time **20 minutes**
Cooking temperature **low**
Cooking time **3–4 hours**
Serves **4**

4 tablespoons **butter**, at room
    temperature
¼ cup **light brown sugar**
½ cup teaspoon **ground
    cinnamon**
grated rind of ½ cup small
    orange
1 tablespoon finely chopped
    candied or drained
    preserved ginger
⅓ cup chopped pitted **dates**
4 large Braeburn or other
    firm **apples**
⅔ cup **cider apple** or **apple
    juice**
hot **custard** or **cream**,
    to serve

Preheat the slow cooker, if necessary; see the manufacturer's instructions. Mix together the butter, sugar, cinnamon, and orange rind until smooth, then stir in the chopped ginger and dates.

Trim a thin slice off the bottom of the apples, if needed, so that they will stand up without rolling over, then cut a thick slice off the top of each and reserve for later. Using a small knife, cut away the apple core to leave a cavity for the stuffing.

Divide the date mixture into 4 and press a portion into each apple cavity, spreading it over the top cut edge of the apple if it won't all fit in. Replace the apple lids and then put the apples into the slow cooker pot. Pour the apple juice into the bottom of the pot, cover with the lid, and cook on low for 3–4 hours or until the apples are tender.

Lift the apples carefully out of the slow cooker and serve in shallow dishes with the sauce spooned over and a drizzle of hot custard or cream.

For baked apples with gingered cherries, follow the recipe as above, but omit the cinnamon, replace the orange rind with lemon rind and replace the dates with ¼ cup chopped candied cherries.

214

compote with mascarpone

Preparation time **20 minutes**
Cooking temperature **high**
Cooking time **1–1¼ hours**
Serves **4**

4 **nectarines**, halved, stoned
  and flesh diced
1½ cups halved or quartered
  strawberries, depending
  on size
¼ cup **superfine sugar**, plus
  2 tablespoons
finely grated rind and juice of
  2 **oranges**
½ cup cold **water**
5 oz **mascarpone cheese**
8 **amaretti cookies**

Preheat the slow cooker, if necessary; see the manufacturer's instructions. Put the nectarines and strawberries in the slow cooker pot with ¼ cup sugar, the rind of 1 orange, the juice of 1½ oranges, and the measured water. Cover and cook on high for 1–1¼ hours or until the fruit is tender. Serve warm or cold.

Just before the compote is ready, mix the mascarpone with the remaining sugar, orange rind and orange juice. Reserve some of the amaretti cookies for decoration. Crumble the rest with your fingertips into the bowl with the mascarpone and stir until mixed. Spoon the fruit into glasses, top with spoonfuls of the orange mascarpone mixture, and decorate with a sprinkling of amaretti cookie crumbs.

For plum & cranberry compote with orange mascarpone, replace the nectarines and strawberries with 1¼ lb plums, quartered and pitted, and 1¼ cups cranberries (no need to thaw if frozen). Increase the sugar to ⅓ cup, then follow the recipe above, using cranberry and raspberry juice instead of water, if liked.

blackberry & apple preserves

Preparation time **20 minutes**
Cooking temperature **high**
Cooking time **4–5 hours**
Makes **four** 13 oz jars

2 lb **cooking apples**, peeled,
  cored, and chopped
4 cups **granulated sugar**
grated rind of 1 **lemon**
2 tablespoons **water** or
  lemon juice
1¾ cups **blackberries**

Preheat the slow cooker, if necessary; see the manufacturer's instructions. Put all the ingredients in the slow cooker pot in the order listed. Cover with the lid and cook on high for 4–5 hours, stirring once or twice during cooking. By the end of the cooking time, the fruit should be thick and pulpy.

Warm 4 clean jars in the bottom of a low oven. Spoon in the jam, place a waxed disk on top, and let cool. Seal each jar with a cellophane jam pot cover and an rubber band, label, and store for up to 2 months in the refrigerator. (The jam's low sugar content means that it does not keep as long as conventional jam and must be kept in the refrigerator.)

For apple, plum & mixed berry preserves, replace half the apples with 1 lb pitted and chopped red plums and half the blackberries with 1 cup raspberries. Cook and store as above.

tangy citrus curd

Preparation time **25 minutes**
Cooking temperature **low**
Cooking time **3–4 hours**
Makes **two** 13 oz jars

½ cup (1 stick) **unsalted butter**
2 cups **superfine sugar**
grated rind and juice of
  2 lemons
grated rind and juice of
  1 orange
grated rind and juice of 1 **lime**
4 **eggs**, beaten

Preheat the slow cooker, if necessary; see the manufacturer's instructions. Put the butter and sugar in a saucepan, add the fruit rinds, then strain in the juice. Heat gently for 2–3 minutes, stirring occasionally, until the butter has melted and the sugar has dissolved.

Pour the mixture into an ovenproof bowl that will fit comfortably in your slow cooker pot. Let cool for 10 minutes, then gradually strain in the eggs and mix well. Cover the bowl with foil, put foil straps (see page 15) in the slow cooker pot, and place the bowl on top. Pour hot water into the cooker pot to come halfway up the sides of the bowl. Cover with the lid and cook on low for 3–4 hours or until the mixture is very thick. Stir once or twice during cooking if possible.

Warm 2 clean jars in the bottom of a low oven. Spoon in the citrus curd, place a waxed disk on top, and let cool. Seal each jar with a screw-top lid or a cellophane jam pot cover and a rubber band, label and store in the refrigerator. Use within 3–4 weeks.

For lemon curd, prepare as above, but omit the orange and lime and use 3 lemons, rather than 2. Cook and store as above.

chilied tomato & garlic chutney

Preparation time **30 minutes**
Cooking temperature **high**
Cooking time **6–8 hours**
Makes **five** 13 oz jars

2 lb **tomatoes**, skinned and
    roughly chopped
1 large **onion**, chopped
2 **cooking apples**, about
    1 lb, peeled, cored, and
    chopped
2 **red bell peppers**, cored,
    seeded, and diced
½ cup **golden raisins**
½ cup distilled **malt vinegar**
2 cups **granulated sugar**
2–3 large mild **red chilies**,
    halved, seeded, and finely
    chopped
6–8 **garlic cloves**, finely
    chopped
1 **cinnamon stick**, halved
½ teaspoon **ground allspice**
1 teaspoon **salt**
black pepper

Preheat the slow cooker, if necessary; see the
manufacturer's instructions. Put all the ingredients
in the slow cooker pot and mix together. Cover with
the lid and cook on high for 6–8 hours or until thick
and pulpy, stirring once or twice.

Warm 5 clean jars in the bottom of a low oven. Spoon
in the chutney, place a waxed disk on top, and let cool.
Seal each jar with a screw-topped lid, then label. Store
in a cool place for up to 2 months. Once opened, store
in the refrigerator.

For spiced green tomato chutney, replace the
tomatoes with 2 lb green tomatoes (chopped but not
skinned) and replace the onion and bell peppers with
3 onions weighing 1 lb in total. Mix the tomatoes and
onions with the cooking apples, vinegar, sugar, chilies,
and salt. Decrease the garlic cloves to 2 and replace
the cinnamon and allspice with 1 teaspoon ground
ginger, 1 teaspoon turmeric, and 1 teaspoon roughly
crushed cloves. Cook and store as above.

pickled plums

Preparation time **20 minutes**
Cooking temperature **high**
Cooking time **2–2½ hours**
Makes **two** 3 cup jars and
  one 2 cup preserving jar

3 cups **white wine vinegar**
2½ cups **superfine sugar**
7 sprigs of **rosemary**
7 sprigs of **thyme**
7 small **bay leaves**
4 sprigs of **lavender** (optional)
4 **garlic cloves**, unpeeled
1 teaspoon **salt**
½ teaspoon **peppercorns**
3 lb firm red **plums**, washed
  and pricked

Preheat the slow cooker, if necessary; see the manufacturer's instructions. Pour the vinegar and sugar into the slow cooker pot, then add 4 sprigs each of the rosemary and thyme and the bay leaves, all the lavender (if used), the garlic cloves, salt, and peppercorns. Cover with the lid and cook on high for 2–2½ hours, stirring once or twice.

Warm the 3 clean jars in the bottom of a low oven. Pack the plums tightly into the jars. Tuck the remaining fresh herbs into the jars. Strain in the hot vinegar, making sure that the plums are completely covered, then seal tightly with rubber seals and jar lids.

Label the jars and let cool. Transfer to a cool, dark pantry and store for 3–4 weeks before using. Once opened, store in the refrigerator.

For pickled shallots, trim a little off the tops and roots of 2½ lb small shallots. Put them in a bowl and cover with boiling water, let soak for 3 minutes, then pour off the water and recover with cold water. Lift the shallots out one at a time and peel off the brown skins. Drain and layer in a second bowl with 2 tablespoons salt. Let stand overnight. Make up the vinegar mixture in the slow cooker as above, but using 2 cups superfine sugar and 1 cup plus 2 tablespoons packed light brown sugar and omitting the lavender. Turn the shallots into a colander and drain off as much liquid as possible. Rinse with cold water, drain and pat dry with paper towels. Pack tightly into warmed jars, adding a few extra herbs. Pour over the hot, strained vinegar, add crumpled wax paper to keep the shallots beneath the surface of the vinegar, and finish as above.

hot mexican coffee

Preparation time **10 minutes**
Cooking temperature **low**
Cooking time **3–4 hours**
Serves **4**

½ cup **unsweetened cocoa powder**
4 teaspoons **instant coffee granules**
4¼ cups boiling **water**
⅔ cup **dark rum**
½ cup **superfine sugar**
½ teaspoon **ground cinnamon**
1 large dried or fresh **red chili**, halved
⅔ cup **heavy cream**

To decorate
2 tablespoons grated **dark chocolate**

Preheat the slow cooker, if necessary; see the manufacturer's instructions. Put the cocoa and instant coffee in a bowl and mix to a smooth paste with a little of the boiling water.

Pour the cocoa paste into the slow cooker pot. Add the remaining boiling water, the rum, sugar, cinnamon and red chili, and mix together. Cover with the lid and cook on low for 3–4 hours until piping hot or until the coffee is required.

Stir well, then ladle into heatproof glasses. Whip the cream until it is just beginning to hold its shape and spoon a little into each glass. Decorate each drink with a little grated chocolate and a dried chilli, if liked.

For hot mocha coffee, reduce the amount of boiling water to 3¾ cups and use 1 teaspoon vanilla extract instead of the rum and chili. Cook as above, then whisk in 1¾ cups milk. Pour into heatproof glasses, top with cream as above, and decorate with a few mini marshmallows.

lemon syrup

Preparation time **10 minutes**

Cooking temperature **high and low**

Cooking time **3–4 hours**

Makes about **20 glasses**

3 **lemons**, washed and thinly sliced

5 cups **granulated sugar**

3¾ cups boiling **water**

4 teaspoons **tartaric acid** or 2 tablespoons **cream of tartar**

Preheat the slow cooker, if necessary; see the manufacturer's instructions. Add the lemon slices to the slow cooker pot with the sugar and boiling water and stir well until the sugar is almost all dissolved. Cover with the lid and cook on high for 1 hour.

Reduce the heat and cook on low for 2–3 hours or until the lemons are almost translucent. Switch off the slow cooker and stir in the tartaric acid. Let cool.

Remove and discard some of the sliced lemons using a slotted spoon. Transfer the syrup and remaining lemon slices to 2 sterilized screw-topped, wide-necked bottles or storage jars. Seal well, label, and store in the refrigerator for up to 1 month.

Dilute the syrup with water in a ratio of 1:3 to make a drink, adding a few of the sliced lemons for decoration, ice cubes, and sprigs of fresh mint or lemon balm, if liked.

For lemon & lime cordial, prepare the syrup using 2 lemons and 2 limes, washed and thinly sliced (instead of 3 lemons). Serve diluted with sparkling mineral water and sprigs of mint.

hot jamaican punch

Preparation time **10 minutes**
Cooking temperature **high** and
 low
Cooking time **3–4 hours**
Serves **6**

juice of 3 **limes**
1¼ cups **dark rum**
1¼ cups **ginger wine**
2½ cups cold **water**
⅓ cup **superfine sugar**

To decorate
1 **lime**, thinly sliced
2 slices of **pineapple**, cored
 but skin left on and cut into
 pieces

Preheat the slow cooker, if necessary; see the manufacturer's instructions. Strain the lime juice into the slow cooker pot and discard the seeds. Add the rum, ginger wine, water, and sugar, cover, and cook on high for 1 hour.

Reduce the heat to low and cook for 2–3 hours, until the punch is piping hot or until you are ready to serve. Stir well, then ladle into heatproof glasses and add a slice of lime and 2 pieces of pineapple to each glass.

For rum toddy, put the grated rind of 1 lemon and 1 orange and the juice of 3 lemons and 3 oranges into the slow cooker. Add ½ cup honey and the sugar. Increase the water to 3 cups and reduce the rum to ⅔ cup. Cook and serve as above.

mulled cranberry & red wine

Preparation time **10 minutes**

Cooking temperature **high and low**

Cooking time **4–5 hours**

Makes **8–10 glasses**

3 cups inexpensive **red wine**
2½ cups **cranberry juice**
½ cup **brandy, rum, vodka,** or **orange liqueur**
½ cup **superfine sugar**
1 **orange**
8 **cloves**
1–2 **cinnamon sticks** (depending on size)

To serve
1 **orange**, cut into segments
2–3 **bay leaves**
few fresh **cranberries**

Preheat the slow cooker, if necessary; see the manufacturer's instructions. Pour the red wine, cranberry juice, and brandy or other alcohol into the slow cooker pot. Stir in the sugar.

Stud the orange segments with a clove. Break the cinnamon sticks into large pieces and add to the pot with the orange pieces. Cover with the lid and cook on high for 1 hour. Reduce the temperature and cook on low for 3–4 hours.

Replace the orange segments with new ones and add the bay leaves and cranberries. Ladle into heatproof glasses, keeping back the fruits and herbs, if liked.

For mulled orange & red wine, prepare the wine as above, but omit the cranberry juice and instead add 1¼ cups orange juice from a carton and 1¼ cups water. Serve decorated with extra herbs and fruit.

index

acknowledgments

Executive Editor Eleanor Maxfield
Senior Editor Charlotte Macey
Executive Art Editor Karen Sawyer
Designer Mark Stevens
Photographer Stephen Conroy
Home Economist Sara Lewis
Props Stylist Liz Hippisley
Senior Production Controller Carolin Stransky

Commissioned photography © Octopus Publishing Group Ltd./Stephen Conroy